Boehm·3

Boehm Test of Basic Concepts • Third Edition

Ann E. Boehm

Examiner's Manual

THE PSYCHOLOGICAL CORPORATION®

A Harcourt Assessment Company

THE PSYCHOLOGICAL CORPORATION®
A Harcourt Assessment Company

Printed in the United States of America

ISBN 0158020839

Please visit our Web site at www.PsychCorp.com. Please go to www.psychcorp.com/catg/pdf/survey.pdf to comment on this or any of our products. Your feedback is important to us.

Acknowledgements

The author would like to thank the many schools, teachers, students, and other individuals who participated in the Boehm–3 development, tryout, and standardization. The results of hundreds of surveys from teachers and other professionals provided many suggestions and constructive criticism that were so helpful in refining the test.

I would like to extend special thanks to Nancy Flores, senior project director, who made sure the art work was what I wanted, the field testing provided the information we needed, and who has been dedicated to Boehm–3 every step of the way.

And many thanks to Terry Hutchings, project director, who came on board during the standardization stage and manual development. Her attention to detail, sense of humor, and sincere care about the project are deeply appreciated.

There are many individuals at The Psychological Corporation with whom I have personally worked who made this revision of the test a rewarding and enjoyable experience for me:

Pat Zureich, senior project director, for her encouragement and careful eye on accuracy and research documentation;

Dawn Dunleavy, supervising editor, who made sure the materials were presented in the most attractive and useful form;

Chuck Wilkins, psychometrics team leader, for his advice and work on statistical analysis and presentation; and

Larry Price, psychometrician, for carrying out the analyses.

Particular thanks are offered to the dedicated group of people who made it possible to develop the Spanish edition of Boehm–3 simultaneously with the English edition: Nancy Flores, Jennifer Lorenzo, Esther Zapata, and Tom Alvarado.

My appreciation is extended to Dr. Joanne Lenke, whose insight on the psychometric properties of Boehm–3 was invaluable, and to the following members of The Psychological Corporation staff including Dr. Aurelio Prifitera, president, and Dr. Carol Lynn Waryas, senior department director, for their support, recommendations, and contributions to the present revision. My thanks also are extended to the many individuals behind the scene who have contributed to the revision:

Stephanie Adams, production manager
Mark Cooley, production specialist
Kelvin Land, senior systems analyst
Patrick Malec, design and composition manager
Lucie Morales, sampling specialist
Carlos Ramirez, sampling specialist
Agnes Stephenson, statistician
Patrick Williams, senior programmer
Dianne Wyatt, sampling specialist
Marian Zahora, designer

My appreciation is extended to Ben Mahan, whose art is so appealing to the children.

The comments and concerns of the bias review panel were both appreciated and important to the development of the revision.

Finally, I would like to thank all those who have used the test with diverse and special populations and sent me the results of their studies. Their information has been invaluable to understanding the concerns of teachers and others working to help children be successful in the classroom.

A.E.B.

Table of Contents

Chapter 1 Overview

Chapter 2 Administration and Scoring

Chapter 3 Planning Intervention

Chapter 4 Development and Standardization of the English Edition

Chapter 5 Development and Standardization of the Spanish Edition

Figures

Tables

Chapter 1
Overview

Purpose

The *Boehm Test of Basic Concepts–Third Edition* (Boehm–3) was designed to assess students' understanding of 50 important concepts they need to know to be successful in school. The concepts tested in Boehm–3 are among the most useful (and frequently occurring) relational concepts that appear in print materials, reading and mathematics curricula, and teachers' verbal instructions for kindergarten, first- and second-grade students. There are two parallel forms of Boehm–3: *Form E* and *Form F*. Each form addresses the same 50 concepts, in the same order, using different contexts.

Boehm–3 can be used to

- identify students who know most concepts, but demonstrate difficulty understanding a few key concepts that can be embedded in instruction;
- identify concepts that need to be targeted for instruction in the classroom, including those needed for problem solving, classroom routines, and activities;
- compare a student's performance to normative information for grade-level peers;
- identify students who may be "at risk" for learning problems and who may need referral to special education for additional testing;
- conduct pre-post testing to help determine a student's progress as a result of teaching or intervention; and
- conduct research.

Boehm–3 results enable you to identify students who may not have had the learning experiences necessary to develop an understanding of key concepts. The normative information, including percentiles, enables you to compare students with their grade-level peers and identify those students who have difficulty understanding basic concepts.

Some of these concepts may not yet have been covered in the kindergarten curriculum. Second graders, however, may know nearly all of the basic concepts tested as a result of classroom teaching or home experiences. This is important because the major use of the test is for instructional screening and ongoing intervention planning. Because there is only one test item for each of the 50 concepts on *Form E* or *Form F* of Boehm–3, the test cannot be considered a criterion-referenced measure for individual concepts. (Three to five items per concept would be desirable.) However, the teacher may establish the criterion number of concepts to be passed after a given period in school; for example, "By the end of kindergarten, the student should respond appropriately to a minimum of 40 of the 50 basic concepts as determined by the teacher." The Boehm–3 may also be used as one of a battery of tests for purposes of assessing readiness or for identifying students who may be "at risk" for learning difficulty.

Boehm–3 includes parallel forms (*Forms E* and *F*) so teachers can use different forms for pre- and post-testing. The two forms can also be used to determine if the student's comprehension of the concept is consistent across multiple contexts. These results can be used to help evaluate the effectiveness of instruction aimed at the development of basic concepts.

Finally, the test can be used for purposes of research. Since the original publication of the *Boehm Test of Basic Concepts* (1971) and the revision, *Boehm Test of Basic Concepts–Revised* (Boehm–R, 1986), considerable research attention has focused on the acquisition of many of the spatial, quantitative, and temporal concepts included on the test. This research points both to the continued importance of basic relational concepts and to the types of problems that students encounter while learning these concepts.

What Basic Concepts Are and Why They Are Important

Basic concepts are words that are used to describe qualities of people or objects *(pretty, tall, angry, small)*, spatial relationships *(in, on, under, beside, in back of)*, time *(before, after)*, and quantity *(more, few, some)*. Quality, spatial, time, and quantity concepts are all concepts that a student needs to know to understand the lessons and instructions the teacher presents in the classroom. Understanding basic concepts is essential for a student to do well in school.

Relational concepts as defined by this test include:

- size *(medium-sized)*
- direction *(away)*
- position in space *(top)*
- quantity *(as many)*
- time *(first)*
- classification *(all)*
- general *(other)*

Basic relational concepts are important to a student's language and cognitive development. They help students understand and describe the world around them and they are a subset of concepts that students use to make relational decisions about persons, objects, and situations. Many relational concepts (e.g., *before* and *after*) cross contexts. Objects can be spoken of as appearing *before* or *after* others in a spatial array ("Point to a girl who is in line *before* a boy"). Events are spoken of in a temporal context, such as *before* or *after* others in a story sequence

("*Before* they went home, they stopped at the store"). In a more general context, a number may be spoken of as occurring *before* or *after* another number in a sequence ("Which number comes *after* 3?"). Generally, these decisions are made in reference to a standard, a dimension, or a situation that can shift. The book on *top* of a pile in one picture may be on the *bottom* in another. Depending on the perspective, the object to the *right* of the student on one occasion can be to the *left* of that student on another occasion.

What Are Basic Concepts?

Basic concepts are words used to describe spatial relationships, time, quantity, and a few others.

For example:

Space:	above, separated, away, over
Time:	never, beginning, before, starting
Quantity:	most, pair, half, widest

Figure 1.1 What Are Basic Concepts?

In contrast to object concepts (e.g., *truck* or *chair*) or color concepts (e.g., *red* and *blue*), it is difficult for a child to form stable internal pictures of basic concepts because their application can change or shift from one situation to another (Boehm 1976, 1982; de Villiers & de Villiers, 1978). A student must be able to apply the same concept across contexts or generalize it to fully understand it (French & Nelson, 1985), which is the basis of difficulty for many students and a challenge for teachers.

Basic concepts are essential thinking tools. They are used at different levels of abstraction to compare, categorize, and solve complex problems. Students need to understand basic concepts to

- understand and describe relationships between and among objects;
- understand the locations and characteristics of persons, places and things;
- understand the order of events;
- follow teacher directions;
- follow instructions in the curriculum areas of language arts, mathematics, and science;
- follow teacher-made and standardized test instructions; and
- engage in problem-solving activities that involve classifying, sequencing, comparing, and identifying multiple attributes.

During the preschool years, children gradually master a variety of basic concepts such as *both, another,* and *before.* As children move from preschool to kindergarten and first grade, knowledge of these basic concepts becomes increasingly critical for understanding what is being communicated in the classroom. For example, the teacher may ask the student to open *both* boxes, find *another* ball, or wash his or her hands *before* eating. Research indicates that many basic concepts are learned during the preschool years (Clark, 1983; de Villiers & de Villiers, 1978; French & Nelson, 1985). However, many concepts are not necessarily part of a child's repertoire when he or she enters kindergarten. Data from the standardization of the Boehm–3 suggest that nearly 50% of kindergartners may not be able to mark the *left* end of the line.

While the authors of preschool, kindergarten, first- and second-grade curricula no longer assume that students entering kindergarten necessarily possess fundamental knowledge of basic concepts, there is great variation in the scope and sequence of basic concept instruction. Often the "Directions" portions of instructional materials, or the teacher in his or her verbal directions, may use such basic concepts as *first, all, begin,* and *before;* often in combination. For example,

> **"*Open* your book to the *first* page."**
>
> **"Find *all* the words that *begin* with the letter *s*."**
>
> **"What number comes *before* 8?"**

Teachers often need to identify and remediate weaknesses in basic concept comprehension at the beginning of the school year and as an ongoing activity. At the preschool level, a teacher can use test results as an indicator of a student's preparedness to cope with school tasks and as a guide for planning instruction in language, emergent literacy, and direction-following behavior. Students experiencing some type of difficulty in learning tend to have more difficulty with basic concepts (Chin, 1975; Kavale, 1982; Nelson & Cummings, 1981; Spector, 1979). Wiig and Semel (1976) suggest that the preschool child who is at risk for learning difficulty is often language delayed, particularly in using adjectives that note aspects of space, time and quantity (basic concepts). Because of growth and rapid learning, preschool children typically show a great deal of day-to-day variability. For this reason, it is important that an early childhood evaluation consist of information obtained from many sources—teachers, parents, direct observation, and assessment tools like the Boehm–3. The Boehm–3 is meant to be used as a tool for planning instruction and is most useful when combined with other information about the child and ongoing teacher observation.

Concept learning tends to be easier or more difficult across different student groups, and often takes place at varying rates. For example, basic concepts present particular difficulty for students with learning disabilities, speech-language difficulties, and other special needs (Caton, 1977; Kavale, 1982). These findings are justifiably a source of concern because of their implications for initial and subsequent school achievement. Research results indicate that students who start out behind tend to stay behind and the gap between average and low achievers tends to widen over time. Because this suggests that the effects of basic concept deficiencies may be cumulative, greater attention is being devoted to instructional activities to close initial gaps in concept learning and language development. In many cases, these gaps may be traceable to a lack of exposure to learning experiences at the preschool level.

Effects of Concept Learning on Standardized Tests

Basic concepts are also part of the directions included in major intelligence tests used at the preschool and early childhood levels, and achievement tests (Bracken, 1986; Cummings & Nelson, 1980; Flanagan, Alfonso, Kaminer, & Rader, 1995; Kaufman, 1978). Lack of familiarity with these basic concepts may affect test performance. Kaufman (1978) reviewed the administrative directions in four widely used ability tests: *Illinois Test of Psycholinguistic Abilities* (Kirk, McCarthy & Kirk, 1982), *McCarthy Scales of Children's Abilities* (McCarthy, 1970), *Stanford-Binet Intelligence Scale* (years II–VII) (Thorndike, Hagen, & Sattler, 1986), and the *Wechsler Preschool and Primary Scale of Intelligence* (WPPSI) (Wechsler, 1967). Various Boehm–3 concepts appeared in the administrative directions of three of the four tests. Easier basic concepts were also included in the tests. Kaufman points out the need for examiners to gain comprehensive knowledge about students' understanding of these concepts and teach them, if necessary, before testing. This point was underscored by McGrew & Flanagan (1998) who reviewed the basic concepts needed to comply with administrative directions of widely used intelligence tests, including the *Differential Ability Scales* (Elliott, 1990), *Kaufman Assessment Battery for Children* (Kaufman & Kaufman, 1983), *Stanford–Binet–IV* (Thorndike, Hagen, & Sattler, 1986), *Wechsler Preschool and Primary Scale of Intelligence Revised* (Wechsler, 1989), and the *Woodcock Johnson–R* (Woodcock & Johnson, 1989).

Goals of the Revision

The original edition of the *Boehm Test of Basic Concepts* was published in 1971 and revised as Boehm–R in 1986. Since that time, there have been many changes in preschool and early school assessment. It is within this context of ongoing research and practice that the *Boehm Test of Basic Concepts* and its subsequent revisions were conceived, and it is to the joint problems of detection and intervention that the test is addressed. The test was devised in a format that can be translated into learning objectives and can be used for curriculum planning and working with parents. The Boehm–3 is compatible with a developmental approach, is derived from the curriculum emphasized during the early years, and its results can be beneficial in planning intervention. Critical reviews and customer feedback indicated that several changes would enhance the usefulness and appropriateness of the test.

Goals for the revision included

- providing updated normative information
- adding a fourth response choice for each item to minimize guessing
- modifying the illustrations to appeal to students taking the test
- increasing the diversity of people pictured in the illustrations including diverse racial groups, individuals in non-stereotypical roles, and differently-abled individuals
- introducing an observation form that teachers and clinicians can use for ongoing observation of the generalized use of basic concepts across curriculum areas
- developing a parent report form to communicate information to parents and provide suggestions for working with their children in the home environment
- developing and standardizing a Spanish edition concurrently with the English edition
- enhancing the transition from one level of Boehm–3 to the other
- improving the overall user friendliness of the test

The brief administration time of the Boehm–R, its ease of administration and scoring, and usefulness for instructional planning have been maintained in the Boehm–3.

Following a careful review of the scope and sequence of concepts tested on Boehm–R, additional concepts were added to Boehm–3. A few new items based on curriculum needs were also added. Items added to the item tryout included *least, ahead, backward, equal*, and *longest*. Some of the concepts tried out for the group-administered version of the test were also tried out in the individually administered preschool level to determine the overlap items that would be included in the preschool level of the test.

Most of the Boehm–R items were modified in some way. Modifications included the addition of a third distractor/foil, instead of two to further decrease guessing. The probability of guessing is now 25% or less (for items with more than four pictures on the page).

All the illustrations are new and in color. Item illustrations are intended to represent the diversity that students see all around them—diverse ethnic and cultural groups, students with different body types, hair colors and textures, and students who wear glasses or use crutches or wheelchairs. Objects and clothing that looked dated were "modernized" based on recommendations by customer survey respondents and/or bias reviewers. Though the illustrations were made more colorful and cartoon-like, it was important that the illustrations be appropriate for second graders and slightly older, developmentally delayed students who are given the test. The amount of detail in the illustrations was kept as simple as possible to keep the pages from looking too busy.

Items are no longer arranged from easy to more difficult. Easy items are interspersed throughout the test to enhance the student's motivation and a sense of success.

Test Components

Boehm–3 is composed of an *Examiner's Manual* with fall and spring norms, *Directions for Administration* (*English* and *Spanish, Forms E* and *F), Forms E* and *F Test Booklets,* and *Forms E* and *F Class Record and Scoring Keys.*

Examiner's Manual

The *Examiner's Manual* contains complete information about the test including administration directions, scoring, interpretation of scores and intervention suggestions, as well as test development, research, and technical information about the normative sample for the English edition. The final chapter provides test development, research, and technical information about the normative sample for the Spanish edition.

Directions for Administration

The *Directions for Administration* (*English* and *Spanish, Forms E* and *F),* include general information, test preparation information, directions for *Forms E* and *F* in both English and Spanish, a reproducible *Test Summary and Teacher Observation Form* in Spanish, and a reproducible *Parent Report Form* in Spanish.

Forms E and F Test Booklets

Two forms of test booklets are available—*Forms E* and *F.* Each of these 20-page booklets include the test stimuli with full-color illustrations, and two perforated forms: the *Test Summary and Teacher Observation Form* and the *Parent Report Form* in English.

Class Record Form and Scoring Key

A *Class Record Form and Scoring Key* is available for each form. Each *Class Record Form and Scoring Key* can accommodate up to 30 students. It can be used to score the test booklet. Spaces are included for each student's raw score, percent correct, performance range, percentile, and a column to note the percentage of students in the class who responded correctly to a particular basic concept.

Administration Time

You may administer the test in one or two sessions. If you administer the test in one session, it may take as long as 45 minutes to administer (10 minutes of which are for preparation). If you need to administer the test in two sessions, each session will require up to 30 minutes (including 10 minutes of preparation).

If you administer the entire test in one test session, you may skip the second set of practice items on page 9 of the test booklet. If you decide to administer the test in two sessions, administer items 1 through 25 in the first test session. Administer practice items *d, e,* and *f,* and test items 26 through 50 in the second test session.

Scores Reported

Boehm–3 results can be reported as a raw score, percent correct, performance range, and a percentile. Total the number of correct responses to get the raw score. Using the raw score, you can determine the percent correct and the performance range. You can also convert the raw score to a percentile. The percentile indicates that the student scored as well as or better than ___% of his or her grade level peers.

User Qualifications

Boehm–3 was designed for use by knowledgeable professionals who have experience in test administration and interpretation, including teachers, speech/language pathologists, special educators, educational diagnosticians, and school psychologists.

How Boehm–3 Assists You in Complying With IDEA Regulations

Boehm–3 (English and Spanish) is a versatile assessment and instructional planning instrument. As part of a comprehensive diagnostic battery of assessment, Boehm–3 is a quick and easy way to assess the student's understanding of the basic concepts needed to succeed in the classroom.

By using key elements of Boehm–3, you are aided in demonstrating compliance with regulations for the Individuals with Disabilities Education Act (IDEA, 1997).

- The *Test Summary and Teacher Observation Form* enables you to document your observations of basic concept use and development and relate it to specific curriculum areas.
- The *Parent Report Form* enables you to inform and involve the parents as partners in helping the student be successful in school.
- You can modify Boehm–3 test materials to assess the basic relational concepts knowledge of older students with special needs. Follow the suggested adaptations and modification of materials that begin on page 14 of this manual.

Other Uses for Boehm–3

Younger students can be screened in small groups using the Boehm–3. This enables teachers and therapists to target key basic concepts for instruction. For children younger than kindergarten age, you may consider using the individually administered *Boehm–3 Preschool* (3-0 to 5-11).

Students from Hispanic backgrounds with English as a second language, or who exhibit limited English proficiency may be assessed by using the identical form in both English and Spanish to determine the degree of their concept development in both languages. As Erickson & Inglesias noted (1989), it is important to assess a child in both languages even when one is dominant, to determine the child's communication abilities and to develop educational plans.

Pre- and post-testing can be conducted using the parallel forms. This can be useful to compare fall and spring skill levels, or to determine the efficacy of teaching or therapeutic intervention.

Limitations

There are some limitations to using Boehm–3 that must be recognized:

- Boehm–3 should never be the only assessment procedure used to determine the placement of a student in a special services program.
- You may use Boehm–3 with students out of the age range represented in the standardization study (students in kindergarten, first, and second grades) to determine their basic concept skills. You may report a raw score as criterion-referenced information about such a student's performance. However, you may not convert the student's raw score to a performance range or a percentile because the standardization sample only included students from kindergarten through second grade.

Chapter 2
Administration and Scoring

General Information

Administering Boehm–3 *Forms E* and *F* is simple and straightforward. Each form consists of a total of 50 pictorial items in one test booklet. Three practice items are presented, followed by 25 test items. There is a break point after the first 25 items if you wish to administer the test in two sessions or give students a brief rest. Three additional practice items appear before items 26 through 50 for those students who would benefit from extra practice. There is considerable advantage in administering the test in separate sessions if the students are very young or lack the attention span required to respond alertly to all 50 items of a form at a single sitting.

Easier items are interspersed with more difficult items in order to increase a student's sense of success and enhance attention. Most students become interested in the test and enjoy taking it, so holding the student's attention, even at the kindergarten level, is usually not difficult. You read the directions to the students, repeat them once, and tell the students to circle the picture that shows his or her answer, exactly as written in the *Directions for Administration.*

Preparing for Testing

Before the initial administration of the test, read this *Examiner's Manual* and review the *Directions for Administration.* Determine which form you want to administer and gather the appropriate number of test booklets for the students and one for yourself. You may write the students' names on the booklets in advance and make a corresponding adjustment in your directions to the students. It may be helpful to have teachers' aides or proctors help the students with writing their names, checking responses to the practice items, turning pages, and finding their place in the test booklet. Each student taking the test must have a pencil or a crayon for marking his/her responses. You may want to have a supply of extra pencils or crayons. If the students use crayons instead of pencils, substitute the word *crayon* for *pencil* when you read the directions.

Classroom Environment

Select a quiet, well lit, well ventilated room that is free of distractions. Before testing, make sure that the students have had a recent bathroom break. Arrange the students so that they sit as far apart as possible. If you are testing very young students unfamiliar with handling and marking pages, consider administering the test to small groups of 8 to 12 students.

Selecting Appropriate Spanish Vocabulary

For students taking the Spanish edition, you will note that the vocabulary used in the Boehm–3 Spanish test items is typical of the vocabulary used in the southwestern United States. Throughout the test, you will find alternate vocabulary words listed as footnotes for specific test items. Before you begin testing, make sure you have reviewed the test items and identified the words that have alternate vocabulary suggestions. Choose the words that are the most familiar to the students in your classroom.

The vocabulary words that Spanish-speaking students recognize can vary, depending on the student's country of origin and the region within that country, the area where the student resides, and the vocabulary he/she uses at home.

Presenting Practice Items

The practice items are included so that you can show the students what they will be expected to do during presentation of the test items. This is your opportunity to verify that each student understands what to do and provide help before the test begins.

During presentation of the *practice* items:

- Help the students locate the icon at the top of the page.
- Make sure the students find the correct practice items on the page.
- Repeat the directions and/or the practice items and provide additional explanation, if needed, until the students know what to do.
- Encourage the students to guess if they do not know the correct answer.
- Tell students the correct answer on the practice items if they do not mark the correct answer after they have guessed.
- Make sure the students have marked the correct answers clearly before beginning the test.
- Try to put the students at ease and make the testing experience pleasant.

Administering Test Items

When you are ready to begin testing, read the directions printed in **bold** aloud to the students. This will give them time to find the correct row of pictures, scan the pictures, and listen to the directions again, if needed. This reduces the memory load for the student. Emphasize the concept words that appear in *italic*. Do not read the item numbers. Read and follow the directions exactly as written.

During presentation of the test items:

- Make sure the students are attentive when you begin to read a test item.
- Read the test items exactly as they appear in the *Directions for Administration*.

- Pause where indicated in the script.
- Make sure the students are attentive and ready to go on before proceeding to the next test item.
- Provide reinforcing statements to encourage the students.
- Encourage the students to guess.

You *may not*

- reword administration directions or test items; or
- cue the students, give them hints, or explain the meaning of the words in the test items.

Answering Students' Questions

During the administration of test items, you may answer students' questions about the mechanics of testing. For example, if a student is unsure about whether he or she is looking at the correct row of pictures, or asks how to circle the answer, you may answer his or her question. However, if a student has a question about the content of a test item (e.g., "Is this one *few?*" or "Does *whole* mean *big?*"), tell the student, **"Draw a circle around the answer you think is best."**

The Page-Finder Icons

Each page of the booklet has a page-finder icon at the top outer corner. These icons are meant to help the students find the correct page. You may use your copy of the test booklet to show students the appropriate place on the page and the picture stimuli for the item you are presenting. Be careful not to point to any particular object within the picture. If students have difficulty keeping their place, they can use a place marker (such as an eraser or ruler placed at the correct row of pictures).

Correcting Mistakes or Changing Answers

If a student makes a mistake and wants to change a response, he or she may erase it or mark an X through the incorrect answer and draw a circle around the new answer.

To Begin Testing

Use the chart below to locate the form you will be administering. The administration directions for that form can be found in the *Directions for Administration* (*English* and *Spanish, Forms E* and *F*) on the pages listed.

Language	Form	Begin Page	End Page
English	E	5	13
	F	13	21
Spanish	E	22	31
	F	32	41

Modification and Adaptation of Test Instructions and/or Materials

Students with special needs may require modifications or adaptations to be able to take the Boehm–3. Any use of modifications and adaptations, however, invalidates the normative information based on a standardized administration of the test. Therefore, performance range and percentile information may not be reported in such cases. Possible modifications or adaptations include:

- presenting fewer test items,
- cutting the booklet apart and presenting a single item at a time for students who use eye gaze or assistive devices to indicate their response,
- placing increased emphasis (highlighting) on key words of test instructions to the student beyond the original test administration directions,
- altering the speed of presentation of the items, and
- utilizing concrete objects in lieu of test booklet stimuli.

Students requiring individual attention to complete testing may benefit from being administered the *Boehm–3 Preschool*, which contains some of the same concepts. Although *Boehm–3 Preschool* was standardized on children ages 3-0 through 5-11, it may be a beneficial measure of older differently-abled students' basic concepts knowledge. Because use of this test with an older student constitutes a modification of the age limits, this would invalidate the *Boehm–3 Preschool* normative information and reporting of performance range and percentile information would not be appropriate.

Instructions for Form E, English

When you are ready to begin testing, say, **"I am going to give each of you a book. Leave it on your desk until I tell you what to do."**

Distribute the *Form E* booklet face up to each student.

Say, **"I have given you a book with some pictures in it. Listen and do just as I say."**

Point to the line at the top of the cover of your test booklet. Say, **"Print your name on the line right here. Then put your pencil down."** If you write the students' names on the test booklets before testing, omit this direction.

Helping Students Identify Page-Finder Icons

When the students have written their names at the top of the first page, say, **"Now find the little box with the *candle* in it. It is up here on your page.** (Hold up a test booklet and show the students where the candle icon is located.) **Did you find it? Put your finger on it."**

Check to see that every student has found the candle. Assist those who are having trouble. When each student has put his or her finger on the candle, say, **"Now take your finger off the little box with the *candle* and pick up your pencil."** Wait until all of the students have responded before beginning the practice items.

Teaching Students to Mark Practice Items and Correct Mistakes

Say, **"We are going to look at boxes that have pictures in them. I am going to tell you to find a picture and draw a circle around it. This is how you draw a circle."** Draw a large circle on the chalkboard.

"I'll tell you to circle a picture, and then I'll say it again, so that everybody has a chance to hear it. Just mark the answer one time."

Administer practice items *a* through *c*. Encourage children to listen carefully and remember to emphasize the italicized words. Provide as much help as the students need to understand the task. (See page 2 of the *Directions for Administration* for complete directions.)

a. Say, **"Now look at the picture with the shoe, the shirt, the pants, and the sock.** (Show the students the correct place on the test booklet.) **Circle the *shirt*.** (Pause and observe the students to make sure you have their attention before repeating the item.) **Circle the *shirt*."**

Wait until all the students have responded. Make sure that all students have circled the shirt. Assist the students who did not circle the shirt. Answer any questions.

b. Say, **"Now look at the things to ride.** (Show the students the correct place on the test booklet.) **Circle the *bicycle*.** (Pause and observe the students.) **Circle the *bicycle*."**

Check the students' responses and assist those who did not circle the bicycle or who marked a picture other than the bicycle.

c. Say, **"Look at the fruit.** (Show the students the correct place on the test booklet.) **Circle the *apple.*** (Pause and observe the students.) **Circle the *apple.*"**

Check the students' responses and assist those who did not circle the apple or who marked a picture other than the apple.

Then say, **"If you make a mistake or want to change an answer, mark a big X on it like this** (demonstrate on the chalkboard). **Then draw a circle around the new answer."**

When you see that everyone has marked his or her answers, say, **"Very good. Now put your pencils down. I will look at your books. Do not turn the page."**

This is your last opportunity to make sure that the students understand the task, as well as how to draw a circle on the form. Make certain that each student has circled the shirt, the bicycle, and the apple. If anyone has marked the wrong answer, point out the error and have the student correct it. If any student has not clearly circled the shirt, bicycle, or apple, show him or her how to do it.

When you have checked all the practice items and the students appear confident that they understand what to do, start reading the test items.

Test Items

Say, **"Now open your book to the next page."**

Open your booklet to page 2 and fold it back so that only page 2 shows. Assist the students if necessary. Then point to the box in the upper left corner of page 2.

Say, **"Look for the little box like this one on your page. Put your finger on the little box with the scissors in it."**

Check to see that each student has found the proper box. Then start reading the test items. *Do not read the item numbers.*

Say, **"Now take your finger off the little box with scissors in it and pick up your pencil."**

1. **"Look at the cats playing.** (Pause until you see that the students have found the correct picture.) **Circle the cat that is at the *top.*** (Pause and observe the students.) **Circle the cat that is at the *top.*"**

2. **"Look at the marbles.** (Pause until you see that the students have found the correct picture.) **Circle the marble that is in the *center* of the box.** (Pause and observe the students.) **Circle the marble that is in the *center* of the box."**

3. **"Look at the cakes.** (Pause until you see that the students have found the correct picture.) **Circle the picture that shows a *whole* cake.** (Pause and observe the students.) **Circle the picture that shows a *whole* cake."**

4. **"Look at the children at the house.** (Pause until you see that the students have found the correct picture.) **Circle the child who is at the *side* of the house.** (Pause and observe the students.) **Circle the child who is at the *side* of the house."**

Hold up your booklet and turn it so that page 3 shows. Tell the students, **"Turn your book over to the next page."** Then point to the box on the upper right corner of page 3. Say, **"Now put your finger on the little box with the pear in it."** Make sure that everyone has found the correct page.

5. **"Look at the children at the drinking fountain.** (Pause until you see that the students have found the correct picture.) **Circle the child who is *last* in line.** (Pause and observe the students.) **Circle the child who is *last* in line."**
6. **"Look at the T-shirts.** (Pause until you see that the students have found the correct picture.) **Circle the T-shirt that is *medium-sized*.** (Pause and observe the students.) **Circle the T-shirt that is *medium-sized*."**
7. **"Look at the box, the feather, the wheel, and the ball.** (Pause until you see that the students have found the correct picture.) **Circle the thing that a bicycle *always* has.** (Pause and observe the students.) **Circle the thing that a bicycle *always* has."**
8. **"Look at the frogs on the log.** (Pause until you see that the students have found the correct picture.) **Circle the frog that is on the *right*.** (Pause and observe the students.) **Circle the frog that is on the *right*."**

Turn your booklet to page 4 and fold it back. Tell the students, **"Turn the page and fold it back."** Then point to the box on the upper left corner of page 4. Say, **"Now put your finger on the little box with the light bulb in it."** Make sure that everyone has found the correct page.

9. **"Look at the eggs that came out of the basket.** (Pause until you see that the students have found the correct picture.) **Circle the egg that is at the *corner* of the table.** (Pause and observe the students.) **Circle the egg that is at the *corner* of the table."**
10. **"Look at the pictures of the boy.** (Pause until you see that the students have found the correct picture.) **Circle the picture that shows the boy *before* he hurt his finger.** (Pause and observe the students.) **Circle the picture that shows the boy *before* he hurt his finger."**
11. **"Look at the pull toy with animals on it.** (Pause until you see that the students have found the correct picture.) **Circle the animal that is at the *end* of the pull toy.** (Pause and observe the students.) **Circle the animal that is at the *end* of the pull toy."**
12. **"Look at the bees and the flower.** (Pause until you see that the students have found the correct picture.) **Circle the bee that is *farthest* from the flower.** (Pause and observe the students.) **Circle the bee that is *farthest* from the flower."**

Turn your booklet so that page 5 shows. Tell the students, **"Turn your book over to the next page."** Then point to the box on the upper right corner of page 5. Say, **"Now put your finger on the little box with the bicycle in it."** Make sure that everyone has found the correct page.

13. **"Look at the pictures of airplanes.** (Pause until you see that the students have found the correct picture.) **Circle the picture that shows only *part* of an airplane.** (Pause and observe the students.) **Circle the picture that shows only *part* of an airplane."**

14. **"Look at the cats playing.** (Pause until you see that the students have found the correct picture.) **Circle the cat that is jumping *through* the window.** (Pause and observe the students.) **Circle the cat that is jumping *through* the window."**

15. **"Look at the plants.** (Pause until you see that the students have found the correct picture.) **Circle the plant with *some, but not many,* flowers.** (Pause and observe the students.) **Circle the plant with *some, but not many,* flowers."**

16. **"Look at the house with the windows.** (Pause until you see that the students have found the correct picture.) **Circle the window that is *above* the door.** (Pause and observe the students.) **Circle the window that is *above* the door."**

Turn your booklet to page 6. Tell the students, **"Turn the page."** Then point to the box on the upper left corner of page 6. Say, **"Now put your finger on the little box with the shoe in it."** Make sure that everyone has found the correct page.

17. **"Look at the pictures of building blocks.** (Pause until you see that the students have found the correct picture.) **Circle the picture where the blocks are *separated.*** (Pause and observe the students.) **Circle the picture where the blocks are *separated.*"**

18. **"Look at the children in line.** (Pause until you see that the students have found the correct picture.) **Circle the child who is *first* in line.** (Pause and observe the students.) **Circle the child who is *first* in line."**

19. **"Look at the pictures of puppies.** (Pause until you see that the students have found the correct picture.) **Circle the picture where all the puppies are in a *row.*** (Pause and observe the students.) **Circle the picture where all the puppies are in a *row.*"**

20. **"Look at the plates of strawberries.** (Pause until you see that the students have found the correct picture.) **Circle the plate that has a *few* strawberries.** (Pause and observe the students.) **Circle the plate that has a *few* strawberries."**

Turn to page 7. Say, **"Turn the page. Now find the little box with the book in it."** Point to the box with the book in it. Make sure that everyone has found the correct page.

21. **"Look at the rabbit, cat, pig, and dog.** (Pause until you see that the students have found the correct picture.) **Circle the animal that is *next to* the rabbit.** (Pause and observe the students.) **Circle the animal that is *next to* the rabbit."**

22. **"Look at the pictures of flowers and bees.** (Pause until you see that the students have found the correct picture.) **Circle the picture that shows a bee on *every* flower.** (Pause and observe the students.) **Circle the picture that shows a bee on *every* flower."**

23. **"Look at the birds.** (Pause until you see that the students have found the correct picture.) **Circle the bird that is at the *bottom* of the tree.** (Pause and observe the students.) **Circle the bird that is at the *bottom* of the tree."**

24. **"Look at the apple, grapes, pear, and chair.** (Pause until you see that the students have found the correct picture.) **Circle the thing a child *never* eats.** (Pause and observe the students.) **Circle the thing a child *never* eats."**

Turn to page 8. Say, **"Turn the page. Now find the little box with the hat in it."** Point to the box with the hat in it. Make sure that everyone has found the correct page.

25. **"Look at the children on the stairs.** (Pause until you see that the students have found the correct picture.) **Circle the child who is *beginning* to climb the stairs.** (Pause and observe the students.) **Circle the child who is *beginning* to climb the stairs."**

Note: If you are going to administer this test in *one* testing session, you may choose to skip the second set of practice items on page 9.

If you have decided to administer this test in *two* testing sessions, you can stop testing here. When you continue testing, administer practice items *d*, *e*, and *f* before presenting items 26 through 50.

Turn to page 9. Say, **"Find the little box with the ice-cream cone in it."** Point to the box with the ice-cream cone in it. Make sure that everyone has found the correct page.

Say, **"Now take your finger off the little box with the ice-cream cone and pick up your pencil."**

Wait until all the students have responded.

d. Say, **"Now look at the picture with the bowl, the glass, the plate, and the fork. Circle the *fork.*** (Pause and observe the students to make sure you have their attention before repeating the practice item.) **Circle the *fork.*"**

Wait until all the students have responded. Make sure that all the students have circled the fork. Assist students who did not circle the fork. Answer any questions.

e. Say, **"Now look at the animals.** (Show the students the correct place on the test booklet.) **Circle the *bird.*** (Pause and observe the students.) **Circle the *bird.*"**

Check the students' responses and assist those who did not circle the bird or who marked a picture other than the bird.

f. Say, **"Look at the furniture. Circle the *chair.*** (Pause and observe the students.) **Circle the *chair.*"**

Check the students' responses and assist those who did not circle the chair or who marked a picture other than the chair.

Then say, **"If you make a mistake or want to change an answer, mark a big X on it like this** (demonstrate on the chalkboard). **Then draw a circle around the new answer."**

When you see that everyone has marked his or her answers, say, **"Very good. Now put down your pencils. I will look at your books. Do not turn the page."**

This is your last opportunity to make sure that the students understand the task, as well as how to draw a circle on the form. Make certain that each student has circled the fork, the bird, and the chair. If anyone has marked the wrong answer, point out the error and have the student correct it. If any student has not clearly circled the fork, bird, or chair, show him or her how to do it.

When you have checked all the work and the students appear confident that they understand what to do, start reading the test items.

Turn to page 10. Say, **"Turn the page. Now find the little box with the fish in it."** Point to the box with the fish in it. Make sure that everyone has found the correct page.

26. **"Look at the house and cars.** (Pause until you see that the students have found the correct picture.) **Circle the *second* car from the house.** (Pause and observe the students.) **Circle the *second* car from the house."**

27. **"Look at the cats and the car.** (Pause until you see that the students have found the correct picture.) **Circle the cat that is in *front* of the car.** (Pause and observe the students.) **Circle the cat that is in *front* of the car."**

28. **"Look at the ties.** (Pause until you see that the students have found the correct picture.) **Circle the tie that is the *widest.*** (Pause and observe the students.) **Circle the tie that is the *widest.*"**

29. **"Look at the ducks and the water.** (Pause until you see that the students have found the correct picture.) **Circle the duck that is *away* from the water.** (Pause and observe the students.) **Circle the duck that is *away* from the water."**

Turn to page 11. Say, **"Turn the page. Now find the little box with the pencil in it."** Point to the box with the pencil in it. Make sure that everyone has found the correct page.

30. **"Look at the pizzas.** (Pause until you see that the students have found the correct picture.) **Circle the picture that shows *half* a pizza.** (Pause and observe the students.) **Circle the picture that shows *half* a pizza."**

31. **"Look at the pictures of puppies.** (Pause until you see that the students have found the correct picture.) **Circle the picture where the puppies are *alike.*** (Pause and observe the students.) **Circle the picture where the puppies are *alike.*"**

32. **"Look at the jars of candy.** (Pause until you see that the students have found the correct picture.) **Circle the jar that has the *fewest* candies.** (Pause and observe the students.) **Circle the jar that has the *fewest* candies."**

33. **"Look at the pictures of shirts and shorts.** (Pause until you see that the students have found the correct picture.) **Circle the picture of the shirt and shorts that *match.*** (Pause and observe the students.) **Circle the picture of the shirt and shorts that *match.*"**

Turn to page 12. Say, **"Turn the page. Now find the little box with the feather in it."** Point to the box with the feather in it. Make sure that everyone has found the correct page.

34. **"Look at the birds and the rainbow.** (Pause until you see that the students have found the correct picture.) **Circle the bird that is flying *over* the rainbow.** (Pause and observe the students.) **Circle the bird that is flying *over* the rainbow."**

35. **"Look at the candies that are in the drawer.** (Point to the drawer. Pause until you see that the students have found the correct picture.) **Circle the picture that has *as many* candies as the drawer.** (Pause and observe the students.) **Circle the picture that has *as many* candies as the drawer."**

36. **"Look at the animals standing in line.** (Pause until you see that the students have found the correct picture.) **Circle the animal that is *third* in line.** (Pause and observe the students.) **Circle the animal that is *third* in line."**

37. **"Look at the desserts. One is ice cream and one is a bowl of grapes.** (Pause until you see that the students have found the correct picture.) **Circle the *other* dessert.** (Pause and observe the students.) **Look at the desserts. One is ice cream and one is a bowl of grapes. Circle the *other* dessert."**

Turn to page 13. Say, **"Turn the page. Now find the little box with the spoon in it."** Point to the box with the spoon in it. Make sure that everyone has found the correct page.

38. **"Look at the man and the ladder.** (Pause until you see that the students have found the correct picture.) **Circle the picture of the man *starting* to climb the ladder.** (Pause and observe the students.) **Circle the picture of the man *starting* to climb the ladder."**

39. **"Look at the boxes of crayons.** (Pause until you see that the students have found the correct picture.) **Circle the box that has the *most* crayons.** (Pause and observe the students.) **Circle the box that has the *most* crayons."**

40. **"Look at the chair and the toys.** (Pause until you see that the students have found the correct picture.) **Circle the toy that is *behind* the chair.** (Pause and observe the students.) **Circle the toy that is *behind* the chair."**

41. **"Look at the dinosaurs.** (Pause until you see that the students have found the correct picture.) **Circle the dinosaur that is on the *left*.** (Pause and observe the students.) **Circle the dinosaur that is on the *left*."**

Turn to page 14. Say, **"Turn the page. Now find the little box with the butterfly in it."** Point to the box with the butterfly in it. Make sure that everyone has found the correct page.

42. **"Look at the pictures of blocks and cars.** (Pause until you see that the students have found the correct picture.) **Circle the picture of the car *between* the blocks.** (Pause and observe the students.) **Circle the picture of the car *between* the blocks."**

43. **"Look at the shirts.** (Pause until you see that the students have found the correct picture.) **Circle the shirt that is *different*.** (Pause and observe the students.) **Circle the shirt that is *different*."**

44. **"Look at the pictures of shoes.** (Pause until you see that the students have found the correct picture.) **Circle the picture that shows a *pair* of shoes.** (Pause and observe the students.) **Circle the picture that shows a *pair* of shoes."**

45. **"Look at the birds flying.** (Pause until you see that the students have found the correct picture.) **Circle the bird that is *below* the cloud.** (Pause and observe the students.) **Circle the bird that is *below* the cloud."**

Turn to page 15. Say, **"Turn the page. Now find the little box with the flower in it."** Point to the box with the flower in it. Make sure that everyone has found the correct page.

46. **"Find the picture of the rocket in the circle.** (Pause until you see that the students have found the correct picture.) ***Skip* a rocket and draw a circle around the next rocket.** (Pause and observe the students.) ***Skip* a rocket and draw a circle around the next rocket."**

47. **"Look at the pictures of the girl.** (Pause until you see that the students have found the correct picture.) **Circle the picture of the girl who is bending *forward*.** (Pause and observe the students.) **Circle the picture of the girl who is bending *forward*."**

48. **"Look at the glasses of juice.** (Pause until you see that the students have found the correct picture.) **Circle the glass with the *least* juice.** (Pause and observe the students.) **Circle the glass with the *least* juice."**

49. **"Look at the rabbit in the box.** (Pause until you see that the students have found the correct picture.) **Draw a circle in the box where the rabbit will be when it jumps *backward*.** (Pause and observe the students.) **Draw a circle in the box where the rabbit will be when it jumps *backward*."**

Turn to page 16. Say, **"Turn the page. Now find the little box with the telephone in it."** Point to the box with the telephone in it. Make sure that everyone has found the correct page.

50. **"Look at the ladybugs on the leaves.** (Point to the leaf at the left. Pause until you see that the students have found the correct picture.) **Circle the leaves that have an *equal* number of ladybugs.** (Pause and observe the students.) **Circle the leaves that have an *equal* number of ladybugs."**

When students have completed item 50, say, **"Now we have finished. Put your pencil down on your desk. Close your book now and I will pick it up."**

Instructions for Form F, English

When you are ready to begin testing, say, **"I am going to give each of you a book. Leave it on your desk until I tell you what to do."**

Distribute the Form F booklet face up to each student.

Say, **"I have given you a book with some pictures in it. Listen and do just as I say."**

Point to the line at the top of the cover of your test booklet. Say, **"Print your name on the line right here. Then put your pencil down."** If you write the students' names on the test booklets before testing, omit this direction.

Helping Students Identify Page-Finder Icons

When the students have written their names at the top of the first page, say, **"Now find the little box with the *candle* in it. It is up here on your page.** (Hold up a test booklet and show the students where the candle icon is located.) **Did you find it? Put your finger on it."**

Check to see that every student has found the candle. Assist those who are having trouble. When each student has put his or her finger on the candle, say, **"Now take your finger off the little box with the *candle* and pick up your pencil."** Wait until all of the students have responded before beginning the practice items.

Teaching Students to Mark Practice Items and Correct Mistakes

Say, **"We are going to look at boxes that have pictures in them. I am going to tell you to find a picture and draw a circle around it. This is how you draw a circle."** Draw a large circle on the chalkboard.

"I'll tell you to circle a picture, and then I'll say it again, so that everybody has a chance to hear it. Just mark the answer one time."

Administer practice items *a* through *c*. Remember to emphasize the italicized words. Provide as much help as the students need to understand the task. (See page 2 of the *Directions for Administration* for more complete directions on practice items.)

a. Say, **"Now look at the picture with the bowl, the glass, the plate, and the fork.** (Show the students the correct place on the test booklet.) **Circle the *fork*.** (Pause and observe the students to make sure you have their attention before repeating the practice item.) **Circle the *fork*."**

Wait until all the students have responded. Make sure that all students have circled the fork. Assist the students who did not circle the fork. Answer any questions.

b. Say, **"Now look at the animals.** (Show the students the correct place on the test booklet.) **Circle the *bird.*** (Pause and observe the students.) **Circle the *bird.*"**

Check the students' responses and assist those who did not circle the bird or who marked a picture other than the bird.

c. Say, **"Look at the furniture.** (Show the students the correct place on the test booklet.) **Circle the *chair.*** (Pause and observe the students.) **Circle the *chair.*"**

Check the students' responses and assist those who did not circle the chair or who marked a picture other than the chair.

Then say, **"If you make a mistake or want to change an answer, mark a big X on it like this** (demonstrate on the chalkboard). **Then draw a circle around the new answer."**

When you see that everyone has marked his or her answers, say, **"Very good. Now put your pencils down. I will look at your books. Do not turn the page."**

This is your last opportunity to make sure that the students understand the task, as well as how to draw a circle on the form. Make certain that each student has circled the fork, the bird, and the chair. If anyone has marked the wrong answer, point out the error and have the student correct it. If any student has not clearly circled the fork, bird, or chair, show him or her how to do it.

When you have checked all the work and the students appear confident that they understand what to do, start reading the test items.

Test Items

Say, **"Now open your book to the next page."**

Open your booklet to page 2 and fold it back so that only page 2 shows. Assist the students if necessary. Then point to the box in the upper left corner of page 2.

Say, **"Look for the little box like this one on your page. Put your finger on the little box with the scissors in it."**

Check to see that each student has found the proper box. Then start reading the test items. *Do not read the item numbers.*

Say, **"Now take your finger off the little box with the scissors in it and pick up your pencil."**

1. **"Look at the children playing on the slide.** (Pause until you see that the students have found the correct picture.) **Circle the child who is at the *top.*** (Pause and observe the students.) **Circle the child who is at the *top.*"**

2. **"Look at the strawberries on the tray.** (Pause until you see that the students have found the correct picture.) **Circle the strawberry that is in the *center* of the tray.** (Pause and observe the students.) **Circle the strawberry that is in the *center* of the tray."**

3. **"Look at the hamburger.** (Pause until you see that the students have found the correct picture.) **Circle the picture that shows a *whole* hamburger.** (Pause and observe the students.) **Circle the picture that shows a *whole* hamburger."**

4. **"Look at the cats and the chair.** (Pause until you see that the students have found the correct picture.) **Circle the cat that is at the *side* of the chair.** (Pause and observe the students.) **Circle the cat that is at the *side* of the chair."**

Hold up your booklet and turn it so that page 3 shows. Tell the students, **"Turn your book over to the next page."** Then point to the box on the upper right corner of page 3. Say, **"Now put your finger on the little box with the pear in it."** Make sure that everyone has found the correct page.

5. **"Look at the horses.** (Pause until you see that the students have found the correct picture.) **Circle the horse that is *last* in line.** (Pause and observe the students.) **Circle the horse that is *last* in line."**

6. **"Look at the fish.** (Pause until you see that the students have found the correct picture.) **Circle the fish that is *medium-sized.*** (Pause and observe the students.) **Circle the fish that is *medium-sized."***

7. **"Look at the faucet, the steering wheel, the doorknob, and the tree.** (Pause until you see that the students have found the correct picture.) **Circle the thing a car *always* has.** (Pause and observe the students.) **Circle the thing a car *always* has."**

8. **"Look at the children on the bench.** (Pause until you see that the students have found the correct picture.) **Circle the child who is on the *right.*** (Pause and observe the students.) **Circle the child who is on the *right."***

Turn your booklet to page 4 and fold it back. Tell the students, **"Turn the page and fold it back."** Then point to the box on the upper left corner of page 4. Say, **"Now put your finger on the little box with the lightbulb in it."** Make sure that everyone has found the correct page.

9. **"Look at the mice.** (Pause until you see that the students have found the correct picture.) **Circle the mouse at the *corner* of the room.** (Pause and observe the students.) **Circle the mouse at the *corner* of the room."**

10. **"Look at the pictures of the shirts.** (Pause until you see that the students have found the correct picture.) **Circle the picture that shows the shirt *before* it got dirty.** (Pause and observe the students.) **Circle the picture that shows the shirt *before* it got dirty."**

11. **"Look at the dogs standing in line.** (Pause until you see that the students have found the correct picture.) **Circle the dog that is at the *end* of the line.** (Pause and observe the students.) **Circle the dog that is at the *end* of the line."**

12. **"Look at the birds and the tree.** (Pause until you see that the students have found the correct picture.) **Circle the bird that is *farthest* from the tree.** (Pause and observe the students.) **Circle the bird that is *farthest* from the tree."**

Turn your booklet so that page 5 shows. Tell the students, **"Turn your book over to the next page."** Then point to the box on the upper right corner of page 5. Say, **"Now put your finger on the little box with the bicycle in it."** Make sure that everyone has found the correct page.

13. **"Look at the pictures of frogs.** (Pause until you see that the students have found the correct picture.) **Circle the picture that shows only *part* of a frog.** (Pause and observe the students.) **Circle the picture that shows only *part* of a frog."**

14. **"Look at the dogs.** (Pause until you see that the students have found the correct picture.) **Circle the dog that is jumping *through* the hoop.** (Pause and observe the students.) **Circle the dog that is jumping *through* the hoop."**

15. **"Look at the jars of bugs.** (Pause until you see that the students have found the correct picture.) **Circle the jar with *some, but not many,* bugs.** (Pause and observe the students.) **Circle the jar with *some, but not many,* bugs."**

16. **"Look at the birds and cat.** (Pause until you see that the students have found the correct picture.) **Circle the bird that is *above* the cat.** (Pause and observe the students.) **Circle the bird that is *above* the cat."**

Turn your booklet to page 6. Tell the students, **"Turn the page."** Then point to the box on the upper left corner of page 6. Say, **"Now put your finger on the little box with the shoe in it."** Make sure that everyone has found the correct page.

17. **"Look at the pictures of beads.** (Pause until you see that the students have found the correct picture.) **Circle the picture where the beads are *separated.*** (Pause and observe the students.) **Circle the picture where the beads are *separated."***

18. **"Look at the students in the lunch line.** (Pause until you see that the students have found the correct picture.) **Circle the child who is *first* in line.** (Pause and observe the students.) **Circle the child who is *first* in line."**

19. **"Look at the pictures of glasses.** (Pause until you see that the students have found the correct picture.) **Circle the picture where the glasses are in a *row.*** (Pause and observe the students.) **Circle the picture where the glasses are in a *row."***

20. **"Look at the pictures of puppies.** (Pause until you see that the students have found the correct picture.) **Circle the picture that has a *few* puppies.** (Pause and observe the students.) **Circle the picture that has a *few* puppies."**

Turn to page 7. Say, **"Turn the page. Now find the little box with the book in it."** Point to the box with the book in it. Make sure that everyone has found the correct page.

21. **"Look at the orange, the grapes, the pear, and the apple.** (Pause until you see that the students have found the correct picture.) **Circle the fruit that is *next to* the apple.** (Pause and observe the students.) **Circle the fruit that is *next to* the apple."**

22. **"Look at the pictures of glasses and spoons.** (Pause until you see that the students have found the correct picture.) **Circle the picture that shows a spoon in *every* glass.** (Pause and observe the students.) **Circle the picture that shows a spoon in *every* glass."**

23. **"Look at the animals.** (Pause until you see that the students have found the correct picture.) **Circle the animal that is at the *bottom*.** (Pause and observe the students.) **Circle the animal that is at the *bottom*."**

24. **"Look at the shirt, shoe, glass, and pants.** (Pause until you see that the students have found the correct picture.) **Circle the thing a child *never* wears.** (Pause and observe the students.) **Circle the thing a child *never* wears."**

Turn to page 8. Say, **"Turn the page. Now find the little box with the hat in it."** Point to the box with the hat in it. Make sure that everyone has found the correct page.

25. **"Look at the children on the tree.** (Pause until you see that the students have found the correct picture.) **Circle the child who is *beginning* to climb the tree.** (Pause and observe the students.) **Circle the child who is *beginning* to climb the tree."**

Note: If you are going to administer this test in *one* testing session, you may choose to skip the second set of practice items on page 9.

If you have decided to administer this test in *two* testing sessions, you can stop testing here. When you continue testing, administer practice items *d, e,* and *f* before presenting items 26 through 50.

Turn to page 9. Say, **"Turn the page. Find the little box with the ice-cream cone in it."** Point to the box with the ice-cream cone in it. Make sure that everyone has found the correct page.

Say, **"Now take your finger off the little box with the ice-cream cone and pick up your pencil."**

Wait until all the students have responded.

d. Say, **"Now look at the picture with the shoe, the shirt, the pants, and the sock.** (Show the students the correct place on the test booklet.) **Circle the *shirt*.** (Pause and observe students to make sure you have their attention before repeating the item.) **Circle the *shirt*."**

Wait until all the students have responded. Make sure that all students have circled the shirt. Assist students who did not circle the shirt. Answer any questions.

e. Say, **"Now look at the things to ride.** (Show the students the correct place on the test booklet.) **Circle the *bicycle.*** (Pause and observe the students.) **Circle the *bicycle.*"**

Check the students' responses and assist students who did not circle the bicycle or who marked a picture other than the bicycle.

f. Say, **"Look at the fruit.** (Show the students the correct place on the test booklet.) **Circle the *apple.*** (Pause and observe the students.) **Circle the *apple.*"**

Check the students' responses and assist students who did not circle the apple or who marked a picture other than the apple.

Then say, **"If you make a mistake or want to change an answer, mark a big X on it like this** (demonstrate on the chalkboard). **Then draw a circle around the new answer."**

When you see that everyone has marked his or her answers, say, **"Very good. Now put down your pencils. I will look at your books. Do not turn the page."**

This is your last opportunity to make sure that the students understand the task, as well as how to draw a circle on the form. Make certain that each student has circled the fork, the bird, and the chair. If anyone has marked the wrong answer, point out the error and have the student correct it. If any student has not clearly circled the fork, bird, or chair, show him or her how to do it.

When you have checked all the work and the students appear confident that they understand what to do, start reading the test items.

Turn to page 10. Say, **"Turn the page. Now find the little box with the fish in it."** Point to the box with the fish in it. Make sure that everyone has found the correct page.

26. **"Look at the animals and the gate.** (Pause until you see that the students have found the correct picture.) **Circle the *second* animal from the gate.** (Pause and observe the students.) **Circle the *second* animal from the gate."**

27. **"Look at the ducks and the girl.** (Pause until you see that the students have found the correct picture.) **Circle the duck that is in *front* of the girl.** (Pause and observe the students.) **Circle the duck that is in *front* of the girl."**

28. **"Look at the windows.** (Pause until you see that the students have found the correct picture.) **Circle the window that is the *widest.*** (Pause and observe the students.) **Circle the window that is the *widest.*"**

29. **"Look at the blocks and the baby.** (Pause until you see that the students have found the correct picture.) **Circle the block that is *away* from the baby.** (Pause and observe the students.) **Circle the block that is *away* from the baby."**

Turn to page 11. Say, **"Turn the page. Now find the little box with the pencil in it."** Point to the box with the pencil in it. Make sure that everyone has found the correct page.

30. **"Look at the pies.** (Pause until you see that the students have found the correct picture.) **Circle the picture that shows *half* a pie.** (Pause and observe the students.) **Circle the picture that shows *half* a pie."**

31. **"Look at the pictures of teddy bears.** (Pause until you see that the students have found the correct picture.) **Circle the picture where the teddy bears are *alike.*** (Pause and observe the students.) **Circle the picture where the teddy bears are *alike."***

32. **"Look at the pictures of stars.** (Pause until you see that the students have found the correct picture.) **Circle the picture that shows the *fewest* stars.** (Pause and observe the students.) **Circle the picture that shows the *fewest* stars."**

33. **"Look at the pictures of clothes.** (Pause until you see that the students have found the correct picture.) **Circle the picture of the clothes that *match.*** (Pause and observe the students.) **Circle the picture of the clothes that *match."***

Turn to page 12. Say, **"Turn the page. Now find the little box with the feather in it."** Point to the box with the feather in it. Make sure that everyone has found the correct page.

34. **"Look at the children and the rope.** (Pause until you see that the students have found the correct picture.) **Circle the child who is going *over* the rope.** (Pause and observe the students.) **Circle the child who is going *over* the rope."**

35. **"Look at this drawer with pencils in it.** (Point to the drawer. Pause until you see that the students have found the correct picture.) **Circle the picture that has *as many* pencils as the drawer.** (Pause and observe the students.) **Circle the picture that has *as many* pencils as the drawer."**

36. **"Look at the tree and the houses.** (Pause until you see that the students have found the correct picture.) **Circle the *third* house from the tree.** (Pause and observe the students.) **Circle the *third* house from the tree."**

37. **"Look at the animals. One is a pig and one is a rabbit.** (Pause until you see that the students have found the correct picture.) **Circle the *other* animal.** (Pause and observe the students.) **Look at the animals. One is a pig and one is a rabbit. Circle the *other* animal."**

Turn to page 13. Say, **"Turn the page. Now find the little box with the spoon in it."** Point to the box with the spoon in it. Make sure that everyone has found the correct page.

38. **"Look at the girl and the fishing pole.** (Pause until you see that the students have found the correct picture.) **Circle the picture of the girl *starting* to fish.** (Pause and observe the students.) **Circle the picture of the girl *starting* to fish."**

39. **"Look at the boxes of buttons.** (Pause until you see that the students have found the correct picture.) **Circle the box that has the *most* buttons.** (Pause and observe the students.) **Circle the box that has the *most* buttons."**

40. **"Look at the bush and the children.** (Pause until you see that the students have found the correct picture.) **Circle the child who is *behind* the bush.** (Pause and observe the students.) **Circle the child who is *behind* the bush."**

41. **"Look at the mice.** (Pause until you see that the students have found the correct picture.) **Circle the mouse that is on the *left*.** (Pause and observe the students.) **Circle the mouse that is on the *left*."**

Turn to page 14. Say, **"Turn the page. Now find the little box with the butterfly in it."** Point to the box with the butterfly in it. Make sure that everyone has found the correct page.

42. **"Look at the pictures of blocks and bears.** (Pause until you see that the students have found the correct picture.) **Circle the picture that has a bear *between* the blocks.** (Pause and observe the students.) **Circle the picture that has a bear *between* the blocks."**

43. **"Look at the cats.** (Pause until you see that the students have found the correct picture.) **Circle the cat that is *different*.** (Pause and observe the students.) **Circle the cat that is *different*."**

44. **"Look at the pictures of gloves.** (Pause until you see that the students have found the correct picture.) **Circle the picture that has a *pair* of gloves.** (Pause and observe the students.) **Circle the picture that has a *pair* of gloves."**

45. **"Look at the spiders.** (Pause until you see that the students have found the correct picture.) **Circle the spider that is *below* the shelf.** (Pause and observe the students.) **Circle the spider that is *below* the shelf."**

Turn to page 15. Say, **"Turn the page. Now find the little box with the flower in it."** Point to the box with the flower in it. Make sure that everyone has found the correct page.

46. **"Find the circle with a star in it.** (Pause until you see that the students have found the correct picture.) ***Skip* a star and draw a circle on the next star.** (Pause and observe the students.) ***Skip* a star and draw a circle on the next star."**

47. **"Look at the pictures of the boy.** (Pause until you see that the students have found the correct picture.) **Circle the boy who is bending *forward*.** (Pause and observe the students.) **Circle the boy who is bending *forward*."**

48. **"Look at the plates of noodles.** (Pause until you see that the students have found the correct picture.) **Circle the plate that has the *least* noodles.** (Pause and observe the students.) **Circle the plate that has the *least* noodles."**

49. **"Look at the frog in the box.** (Point to the frog in the box. Pause until you see that the students have found the correct picture.) **Draw a circle in the box where the frog will be after it jumps *backward.*** (Pause and observe the students.) **Draw a circle in the box where the frog will be after it jumps *backward.*"**

Turn to page 16. Say, **"Turn the page. Now find the little box with the telephone in it."** Point to the box with the telephone in it. Make sure that everyone has found the correct page.

50. **"Look at these hands holding candies.** (Pause until you see that the students have found the correct picture.) **Circle the hands that are holding an *equal* number of candies.** (Pause and observe the students.) **Circle the hands that are holding an *equal* number of candies."**

When the students have completed item 50, say, **"Now we have finished. Put your pencil down on your desk. Close your book now and I will pick it up."**

Instructions for Form E, Spanish

When you are ready to begin testing, say, **"Les voy a dar un folleto a cada uno. Déjenlo en el escritorio hasta que yo les diga lo que tienen que hacer".**

Distribute the *Form E* booklet face up to each student.

Say, **"Les he dado un folleto con dibujos. Escuchen y hagan lo que yo les diga".**

Point to the line at the top of the cover of your test booklet. Say, **"Escriban su nombre en la línea de la derecha, aquí. Después dejen su lápiz sobre el escritorio".** (If you write the students' names on the test booklets before testing, omit this direction.)

Helping Students Identify Page-Finder Icons

When the students have written their names at the top of the first page, say, **"Ahora, busquen el cuadrito que tiene la candela adentro. Está aquí, en la esquina superior de su página.** (Hold up a test booklet and show the students where the candle icon is located.) **¿Lo encontraron? Pongan su dedo en él".**

Check to see that every student has found the candle. Assist those who are having trouble. When each student has put his or her finger on the candle, say, **"Ahora quiten el dedo del cuadrito que tiene la candela y tomen su lápiz".** Wait until all of the students have responded before beginning the practice items.

Teaching Students to Mark Practice Items and Correct Mistakes

Say, **"Vamos a ver los cuadritos que tienen dibujos adentro. Yo les voy a decir que busquen un dibujo y lo encierren en un círculo. Así se hace un círculo".** Draw a large circle on the chalkboard.

"Les voy a decir que encierren en un círculo un dibujo, y lo voy a decir dos veces para que todos puedan oirlo. Ustedes marcarán la respuesta una sola vez".

Administer practice items *a* through *c*. Remember to emphasize the italicized words. Provide as much help as the students need to understand the task (see page 2 of the *Directions for Administration*).

a. Say, **"Miren el dibujo que tiene el zapato, la camisa, los pantalones y el calcetín.** (Show the students the correct place on the test booklet.) **Encierren en un círculo *la camisa.*** (Pause and observe the students to make sure you have their attention before repeating the item.) **Encierren en un círculo *la camisa".***

Wait until all the students have responded. Make sure that all students have circled the shirt. Assist students who did not circle the shirt. Answer any questions.

b. Say, **"Miren las cosas que se pueden montar.** (Show the students the correct place on the test booklet.) **Encierren en un círculo la *bicicleta.*** (Pause and observe the students.) **Encierren en un círculo la *bicicleta".***

Check the students' responses and assist those who did not circle the bicycle or who marked a picture other than the bicycle.

c. Say, **"Miren las frutas.** (Show the students the correct place on the test booklet.) **Encierren en un círculo la *manzana*.** (Pause and observe the students.) **Encierren en un círculo la *manzana*".**

Check the students' responses and assist those who did not circle the apple or who marked a picture other than the apple.

Then say, **"Si se equivocan o quieren cambiar una respuesta, táchenla con una X grande, así** (demonstrate on the chalkboard), **y después encierren en un círculo la nueva respuesta".**

When you see that everyone has marked his or her answers, say, **"Muy bien. Ahora dejen su lápiz en el escritorio. Voy a ver sus folletos. No vuelvan la página".**

This is your last opportunity to make sure that the students understand the task, as well as how to draw a circle on the form. Make certain that each student has circled the shirt, the bicycle, and the apple. If anyone has marked the wrong answer, point out the error and have the student correct it. If any student has not clearly circled the shirt, bicycle, or apple, show him or her how to do it.

When all the work has been checked and the students appear confident that they understand what to do, start reading the test items.

Test Items

Say, **"Ahora pasen a la página siguiente".**

Open your booklet to page 2 and fold it back so that only page 2 shows. Assist the students if necessary. Then point to the box in the upper left corner of page 2.

Say, **"Busquen un cuadrito como éste en su página. Pongan su dedo en el cuadrito que tiene unas tijeras adentro".**

Check to see that each student has found the proper box. Then start reading the test items. *Do not read the item numbers.*

Say, **"Ahora quiten el dedo del cuadrito que tiene las tijeras adentro y tomen su lápiz".**

1. **"Miren los gatos jugando.** (Pause until you see that the students have found the correct picture.) **Encierren en un círculo el gato que está en lo *más alto*.** (Pause and observe the students.) **Encierren en un círculo el gato que está en lo *más alto*".**
2. **"Miren las canicas.** (Pause until you see that the students have found the correct picture.) **Encierren en un círculo la canica que está en *el centro* del cuadro.** (Pause and observe the students.) **Encierren en un círculo la canica que está en *el centro* del cuadro".**

3. **"Miren los queques.**[1] (Pause until you see that the students have found the correct picture.) **Encierren en un círculo el dibujo de un queque *completo.*** (Pause and observe the students.) **Encierren en un círculo el dibujo de un queque *completo".***

4. **"Miren las personas que están alrededor de la casa.** (Pause until you see that the students have found the correct picture.) **Encierren en un círculo la persona que está *al lado* de la casa.** (Pause and observe the students.) **Encierren en un círculo la persona que está *al lado* de la casa".**

Hold up your booklet and turn it so that page 3 shows. Tell the students, **"Pasen a la página siguiente".** Then point to the box on the upper right corner of page 3. Say, **"Ahora pongan su dedo en el cuadrito que tiene una pera adentro".** Make sure that everyone has found the correct page.

5. **"Miren los niños que están frente a la fuente de agua.** (Pause until you see that the students have found the correct picture.) **Encierren en un círculo el *último* niño de la fila.** (Pause and observe the students.) **Encierren en un círculo el *último* niño de la fila".**

6. **"Miren las camisetas.** (Pause until you see that the students have found the correct picture.) **Encierren en un círculo la camiseta de tamaño *medi-ano.*** (Pause and observe the students.) **Encierren en un círculo la camiseta de tamaño *mediano".***

7. **"Miren la caja, la pluma, la rueda**[2] **y la bola.**[3] (Pause until you see that the students have found the correct picture.) **Encierren en un círculo algo que *siempre* tiene una bicicleta.** (Pause and observe the students.) **Encierren en un círculo algo que *siempre* tiene una bicicleta".**

8. **"Miren las ranas y el tronco.** (Pause until you see that the students have found the correct picture.) **Encierren en un círculo la rana que está a la *derecha.*** (Pause and observe the students.) **Encierren en un círculo la rana que está a la *derecha".***

Turn your booklet to page 4 and fold it back. Tell the students, **"Pasen a la página siguiente".** Then point to the box on the upper left corner of page 4. Say, **"Ahora pongan su dedo en el cuadrito que tiene un foco**[4] **adentro".** Make sure that everyone has found the correct page.

9. **"Miren los huevos que están fuera de la canasta.** (Pause until you see that the students have found the correct picture.) **Encierren en un círculo el huevo que está en la *esquina* de la mesa.** (Pause and observe the students.) **Encierren en un círculo el huevo que está en la *esquina* de la mesa".**

---

[1] Variation: *pasteles, tortas, pan dulce, postres*

[2] Variation: *llanta*

[3] Variation: *pelota*

[4] Variation: *una bujía, una bombilla*

10. **"Miren los dibujos del niño.** (Pause until you see that the students have found the correct picture.) **Encierren en un círculo el dibujo que muestra al niño *antes* de haberse herido[5] el dedo.** (Pause and observe the students.) **Encierren en un círculo el dibujo que muestra al niño *antes* de haberse herido el dedo".**

11. **"Miren el tren de juquete con los animales.** (Pause until you see that the students have found the correct picture.) **Encierren en un círculo el animal que está al *final* del tren.** (Pause and observe the students.) **Encierren en un círculo el animal que está al *final* del tren".**

12. **"Miren la flor y las abejas[6]** (Pause until you see that the students have found the correct picture.) **Encierren en un círculo la abeja que está *más lejos* de la flor.** (Pause and observe the students.) **Encierren en un círculo la abeja que está *más lejos* de la flor".**

Turn your booklet so that page 5 shows. Tell the students, **"Pasen a la página siguiente".** Then point to the box on the upper right corner of page 5. Say, **"Ahora pongan su dedo en el cuadrito que tiene una bicicleta adentro".** Make sure that everyone has found the correct page.

13. **"Miren los dibujos de los aviones.** (Pause until you see that the students have found the correct picture.) **Encierren en un círculo el dibujo que muestra sólo una *parte* del avión.** (Pause and observe the students.) **Encierren en un círculo el dibujo que muestra sólo una *parte* del avión".**

14. **"Miren los gatos jugando.** (Pause until you see that the students have found the correct picture.) **Encierren en un círculo el gato que está pasando *a través* de la ventana.** (Pause and observe the students.) **Encierren en un círculo el gato que está pasando *a través* de la ventana".**

15. **"Miren las plantas[7] con flores.** (Pause until you see that the students have found the correct picture.) **Encierren en un círculo la planta que tiene *algunas, pero no muchas,* flores.** (Pause and observe the students.) **Encierren en un círculo la planta que tiene *algunas, pero no muchas,* flores".**

16. **"Miren la casa con las ventanas.** (Pause until you see that the students have found the correct picture.) **Encierren en un círculo la ventana que está *arriba* de la puerta.** (Pause and observe the students.) **Encierren en un círculo la ventana que está *arriba* de la puerta".**

Turn your booklet to page 6 and fold it back. Tell the students, **"Pasen a la página siguiente".** Then point to the box on the upper left corner of page 6. Say, **"Ahora pongan su dedo en el cuadrito que tiene un zapato adentro".** Make sure that everyone has found the correct page.

[5]Variation: *golpeado*

[6]Variation: *avispas*

[7]Variation: *matas*

17. **"Miren los dibujos de los bloques.** (Pause until you see that the students have found the correct picture.) **Encierren en un círculo el dibujo donde los bloques están *separados.*** (Pause and observe the students.) **Encierren en un círculo el dibujo donde los bloques están *separados".***

18. **"Miren los niños que están en la fila.** (Pause until you see that the students have found the correct picture.) **Encierren en un círculo el *primer* niño de la fila.** (Pause and observe the students.) **Encierren en un círculo el *primer* niño de la fila".**

19. **"Miren los dibujos de los perritos.** (Pause until you see that the students have found the correct picture.) **Encierren en un círculo el dibujo donde todos los perritos están en *línea.*** (Pause and observe the students.) **Encierren en un círculo el dibujo donde todos los perritos están en *línea".***

20. **"Miren el plato de fresas.** (Pause until you see that the students have found the correct picture.) **Encierren en un círculo el plato que tiene *pocas* fresas.** (Pause and observe the students.) **Encierren en un círculo el plato que tiene *pocas* fresas".**

Turn to page 7. Say, **"Pasen a la página siguiente. Ahora busquen el cuadrito que tiene un libro adentro".** Point to the box with the book in it. Make sure that everyone has found the correct page.

21. **"Miren el conejo, el gato, el cerdo[8] y el perro.** (Pause until you see that the students have found the correct picture.) **Encierren en un círculo el animal que está *más cerca* del conejo.** (Pause and observe the students.) **Encierren en un círculo el animal que está *más cerca* del conejo".**

22. **"Miren los dibujos de las flores y las abejas.**[9] (Pause until you see that the students have found the correct picture.) **Encierren en un círculo el dibujo que tiene una abeja en *cada* flor.** (Pause and observe the students.) **Encierren en un círculo el dibujo que tiene una abeja en *cada* flor".**

23. **"Miren los pájaros.** (Pause until you see that the students have found the correct picture.) **Encierren en un círculo el pájaro que está *más abajo* del árbol.** (Pause and observe the students.) **Encierren en un círculo el pájaro que está *más abajo* del árbol".**

24. **"Miren la manzana, las uvas, la pera y la silla.** (Pause until you see that the students have found the correct picture.) **Encierren en un círculo algo que *nunca* come un niño.** (Pause and observe the students.) **Encierren en un círculo algo que *nunca* come un niño".**

---

[8] Variation: *puerco, cochino, marrano, chancho*

[9] Variation: *avispas*

Turn to page 8. Say, **"Pasen a la página siguiente. Ahora busquen el cuadrito que tiene el sombrero adentro".** Point to the box with the hat in it. Make sure that everyone has found the correct page.

25. **"Miren los niños que están en las gradas.**[10] (Pause until you see that the students have found the correct picture.) **Encierren en un círculo el niño que está *empezando* a subir las gradas.** (Pause and observe the students.) **Encierren en un círculo el niño que está *empezando* a subir las gradas".**

Note: If you are going to administer this test in *one* testing session, you may chose to skip the second set of practice items on page 9.

If you have decided to administer this test in *two* testing sessions, you can stop testing here. When you continue testing, administer Practice items *d, e,* and *f* before presenting items 26 through 50.

Turn to page 9. Say, **"Pasen a la página siguiente. Ahora busquen el cuadrito que tiene el helado**[11] **adentro".** Point to the box with the ice-cream cone in it. Make sure that everyone has found the correct page.

Say, **"Ahora quiten el dedo del cuadrito que tiene el helado adentro y tomen su lápiz".**

Wait until all the students have responded.

d. Say, **"Miren el dibujo del tazón,**[12] **el vaso, el plato y el tenedor. Encierren en un círculo el *tenedor.*** (Pause and observe the students to make sure you have their attention before repeating the practice item.) **Encierren en un círculo el *tenedor".***

Wait until all the students have responded. Make sure that all the students have circled the fork. Assist students who did not circle the fork. Answer any questions.

e. Say, **"Ahora, miren los animales.** (Pause and observe the students.) **Encierren en un círculo el *pájaro".***

Check the students' responses and assist those who did not circle the bird or who marked a picture other than the bird.

Say, **"Miren los muebles. Encierren en un círculo la *silla.*** (Pause and observe the students.) **Encierren en un círculo la *silla".***

Check the students' responses and assist those who did not circle the chair or who marked a picture other than the chair.

---

[10] Variation: *escalones*

[11] Variation: *sorbete*

[12] Variation: *la sopera*

Then say, **"Si se equivocan o quieren cambiar una respuesta, táchenla con una X grande, así** (demonstrate on the chalkboard) **y después encierren en un círculo la nueva respuesta".**

When you see that everyone has marked his or her answers, say, **"Muy bien. Ahora dejen su lápiz en el escritorio. Voy a ver sus folletos. No vuelvan la página".**

This is your last opportunity to make sure that the students understand the task, as well as how to draw a circle on the form. Make certain that each student has circled the fork, the bird, and the chair. If anyone has marked the wrong answer, point out the error and have the student correct it. If any student has not clearly circled the fork, bird, or chair, show him or her how to do it.

When you have checked all the work and the students appear confident that they understand what to do, start reading the test items.

Turn to page 10. Say, **"Pasen a la página siguiente. Ahora busquen el cuadrito que tiene un pescadito adentro".** Point to the box with the fish in it. Make sure that everyone has found the correct page.

26. **"Miren la casa y los carros.** (Pause until you see that the students have found the correct picture.) **Encierren en un círculo el *segundo* carro a partir de la casa.** (Pause and observe the students.) **Encierren en un círculo el *segundo* carro a partir de la casa".**

27. **"Miren los gatos y el carro.** (Pause until you see that the students have found the correct picture.) **Encierren en un círculo el gato que está *en frente* del carro.** (Pause and observe the students.) **Encierren en un círculo el gato que está *en frente* del carro".**

28. **"Miren las corbatas.** (Pause until you see that the students have found the correct picture.) **Encierren en un círculo la corbata *más ancha.*** (Pause and observe the students.) **Encierren en un círculo la corbata *más ancha".***

29. **"Miren los patos y el agua.** (Pause until you see that the students have found the correct picture.) **Encierren en un círculo el pato que está *retirado* del agua.** (Pause and observe the students.) **Encierren en un círculo el pato que está *retirado* del agua".**

Turn to page 11. Say, **"Pasen a la página siguiente. Ahora busquen el cuadrito que tiene un lápiz adentro".** Point to the box with the pencil in it. Make sure that everyone has found the correct page.

30. **"Miren las pizzas.** (Pause until you see that the students have found the correct picture.) **Encierren en un círculo el dibujo que muestra la *mitad* de una pizza.** (Pause and observe the students.) **Encierren en un círculo el dibujo que muestra la *mitad* de una pizza".**

31. **"Miren los dibujos de los perritos.** (Pause until you see that the students have found the correct picture.) **Encierren en un círculo el dibujo donde los perritos son *iguales.*** (Pause and observe the students.) **Encierren en un círculo el dibujo donde los perritos son *iguales".***

32. **"Miren el frasco con dulces.**[13] (Pause until you see that the students have found the correct picture.) **Encierren en un círculo el frasco que tiene *la menor cantidad* de dulces.** (Pause and observe the students.) **Encierren en un círculo el frasco que tiene *la menor cantidad* de dulces".**

33. **"Miren los dibujos de camisas y pantalones cortos.** (Pause until you see that the students have found the correct picture.) **Encierren en un círculo el dibujo de las camisas y pantalones cortos que *hacen juego*.**[14] (Pause and observe the students.) **Encierren en un círculo el dibujo de las camisas y pantalones cortos que *hacen juego*".**

Turn to page 12. Say, **"Pasen a la página siguiente. Ahora busquen el cuadrito que tiene una pluma adentro".** Point to the box with the feather in it. Make sure that everyone has found the correct page.

34. **"Miren los pájaros y el arcoiris.** (Pause until you see that the students have found the correct picture.) **Encierren en un círculo el pájaro que está volando *sobre* el arcoiris.** (Pause and observe the students.) **Encierren en un círculo el pájaro que está volando *sobre* el arcoiris".**

35. **"Miren los dulces que están en la gaveta.** (Point to the drawer. Pause until you see that the students have found the correct picture.) **Encierren en un círculo el dibujo que tiene *tantos* dulces *como* hay en la gaveta.** (Pause and observe the students.) **Encierren en un círculo el dibujo que tiene *tantos* dulces *como* hay en la gaveta".**

36. **"Miren los animales que están en fila.** (Pause until you see that the students have found the correct picture.) **Encierren en un círculo el *tercer* animal de la fila.** (Pause and observe the students.) **Encierren en un círculo el *tercer* animal de la fila".**

37. **"Miren los postres. Uno es un helado**[15] **y el otro es un tazón**[16] **de uvas.** (Pause until you see that the students have found the correct picture.) **Encierren en un círculo el *otro* postre.** (Pause and observe the students.) **Encierren en un círculo el *otro* postre".**

Turn to page 13. Say, **"Pasen a la página siguiente. Ahora busquen el cuadrito que tiene una cuchara adentro".** Point to the box with the spoon in it. Make sure that everyone has found the correct page.

---

[13] Variation: *caramelos*

[14] Variation: *hacen pareja*

[15] Variation: *sorbete*

[16] Variation: *la sopera*

38. **"Miren los dibujos del hombre y la escalera.** (Pause until you see that the students have found the correct picture.) **Encierren en un círculo el dibujo donde el hombre está *empezando* a subir la escalera.** (Pause and observe the students.) **Encierren en un círculo el dibujo donde el hombre está *empezando* a subir la escalera".**

39. **"Miren las cajas de crayones.**[17] (Pause until you see that the students have found the correct picture.) **Encierren en un círculo la caja que tiene *más* crayones.** (Pause and observe the students.) **Encierren en un círculo la caja que tiene *más* crayones".**

40. **"Miren el sillón y los juguetes.** (Pause until you see that the students have found the correct picture.) **Encierren en un círculo el juguete que está *detrás* del sillón.** (Pause and observe students.) **Encierren en un círculo el juguete que está *detrás* del sillón".**

41. **"Miren los dinosaurios.** (Pause until you see that the students have found the correct picture.) **Encierren en un círculo el dinosaurio que está a la *izquierda.*** (Pause and observe the students.) **Encierren en un círculo el dinosaurio que está a la *izquierda".***

Turn to page 14. Say, **"Pasen a la página siguiente. Ahora busquen el cuadrito que tiene una mariposa adentro".** Point to the box with the butterfly in it. Make sure that everyone has found the correct page.

42. **"Miren los dibujos de los bloques y los carros.** (Pause until you see that the students have found the correct picture.) **Encierren en un círculo el dibujo que tiene un carro *en medio de* dos bloques.** (Pause and observe the students.) **Encierren en un círculo el dibujo que tiene un carro *en medio de* dos bloques".**

43. **"Miren las camisas.** (Pause until you see that the students have found the correct picture.) **Encierren en un círculo la camisa que es *diferente.*** (Pause and observe the students.) **Encierren en un círculo la camisa que es *diferente".***

44. **"Miren los dibujos de los zapatos.** (Pause until you see that the students have found the correct picture.) **Encierren en un círculo el dibujo que muestra un *par* de zapatos.** (Pause and observe the students.) **Encierren en un círculo el dibujo que muestra un *par* de zapatos".**

45. **"Miren los pájaros volando.** (Pause until you see that the students have found the correct picture.) **Encierren en un círculo el pájaro que está *debajo* de la nube.** (Pause and observe the students.) **Encierren en un círculo el pájaro que está *debajo* de la nube".**

[17] Variation: *crayolas*

Turn to page 15. Say, **"Pasen a la página siguiente. Ahora busquen el cuadrito que tiene una flor adentro".** Point to the box with the flower in it. Make sure that everyone has found the correct page.

46. **"Encuentren el dibujo que tiene un cohete dentro de un círculo.** (Pause until you see that the students have found the correct picture.) ***Sáltense*** **un cohete y hagan un círculo en el siguiente cohete.** (Pause and observe the students.) **Encuentren el dibujo que tiene un cohete dentro de un círculo.** ***Sáltense*** **un cohete y hagan un círculo en el siguiente cohete".**

47. **"Miren los dibujos de la niña.** (Pause until you see that the students have found the correct picture.) **Encierren en un círculo el dibujo donde la niña está** ***inclinada*** **hacia adelante.** (Pause and observe the students.) **Encierren en un círculo el dibujo donde la niña está** ***inclinada*** **hacia adelante".**

48. **"Miren los vasos con jugo.** (Pause until you see that the students have found the correct picture.) **Encierren en un círculo el vaso que tiene** ***menos*** **jugo.** (Pause and observe the students.) **Encierren en un círculo el vaso que tiene** ***menos*** **jugo".**

49. **"Miren el conejo que está dentro del cuadrito.** (Pause until you see that the students have found the correct picture.) **Hagan un círculo en el cuadrito donde quedará el conejo después de saltar un espacio** ***hacia atrás.*** (Pause and observe the students.) **Hagan un círculo en el cuadrito donde quedará el conejo después de saltar un espacio** ***hacia atrás".***

Turn to page 16. Say, **"Pasen a la página siguiente. Ahora busquen el cuadrito que tiene un teléfono adentro".** Point to the box with the telephone in it. Make sure that everyone has found the correct page.

50. **"Miren los insectos que están en las hojas.** (Point to the leaf at the left. Pause until you see that the students have found the correct picture.) **Encierren en un círculo las hojas que tienen** ***igual*** **número de insectos.** (Pause and observe the students.) **Encierren en un círculo las hojas que tienen** ***igual*** **número de insectos".**

When students have completed item 50, say, **"Ya terminamos. Dejen sus lápices sobre el escritorio. Cierren sus folletos y yo los voy a recoger".**

Instructions for Form F, Spanish

When you are ready to begin testing, say, **"Les voy a dar un folleto a cada uno. Déjenlo en el escritorio hasta que yo les diga lo que tienen que hacer".**

Distribute the *Form F* booklet face up to each student.

Say, **"Les he dado un folleto con dibujos. Escuchen y hagan lo que yo les diga".**

Point to the line at the top of the cover of your test booklet. Say, **"Escriban su nombre en la línea de la derecha, aquí. Después dejen su lápiz sobre el escritorio".** (If you write the students' names on the test booklets before testing, omit this direction.)

Helping Students Identify the Page-Finder Icons

When the students have written their names at the top of the first page, say, **"Ahora, busquen el cuadrito que tiene la candela adentro. Está aquí, en la esquina superior de su página.** (Hold up a test booklet and show the students where the candle icon is located.) **¿Lo encontraron? Pongan su dedo en él".**

Check to see that every student has found the candle. Assist those who are having trouble. When each student has put his or her finger on the candle, say, **"Ahora quiten el dedo del cuadrito que tiene la candela y tomen su lápiz".** Wait until all of the students have responded before beginning the practice items.

Teaching Students to Mark Practice Items and Correct Mistakes

Say, **"Vamos a ver los cuadritos que tienen dibujos adentro. Yo les voy a decir que busquen un dibujo y le hagan un círculo alrededor. Así se hace un círculo".** Draw a large circle on the chalkboard.

"Yo les voy a decir que hagan un círculo alrededor de un dibujo, y lo voy a repetir para que todos puedan oirlo. Ustedes marcarán la respuesta una sola vez".

Administer practice items *a* through *c*. Remember to emphasize the italicized words. Provide as much help as the students need to understand the task (see page 2 of the *Directions for Administration*).

a. Say, **"Miren el dibujo del tazón, el vaso, el plato y el tenedor. Encierren en un círculo el *tenedor*.** (Pause and observe the students to make sure you have their attention before repeating the practice item.) **Encierren en un círculo el *tenedor*".**

Wait until all the students have responded. Make sure that all students have circled the fork. Assist the students who did not circle the fork. Answer any questions.

b. Say, **"Miren los animales.** (Show the students the correct place on the test booklet.) **Encierren en un círculo el *pájaro*.** (Pause and observe the students.) **Encierren en un círculo el *pájaro*".**

Check the students' responses and assist those who did not circle the bird or who marked a picture other than the bird.

c. Say, **"Miren los muebles.** (Show the students the correct place on the test booklet.) **Encierren en un círculo la *silla.*** (Pause and observe the students.) **Encierren en un círculo la *silla".***

Check the students' responses and assist those who did not circle the apple or who marked a picture other than the apple.

Then say, **"Si se equivocan o quieren cambiar una respuesta, táchenla con una X grande, así** (demonstrate on the chalkboard) **y después encierren en un círculo la nueva respuesta".**

When you see that everyone has marked his or her answers, say, **"Muy bien. Ahora dejen su lápiz en el escritorio. Voy a ver sus folletos. No vuelvan la página".**

This is your last opportunity to make sure that the students understand the task, as well as how to draw a circle on the form. Make certain that each student has has circled the fork, the bird, and the chair. If anyone has marked the wrong answer, point out the error and have the student correct it. If any student has not clearly circled the fork, the bird, and the chair, show him or her how to do it.

When all the work has been checked and the students appear confident that they understand what to do, start reading the test items.

Test Items

Say, **"Ahora pasen a la página siguiente".**

Open your booklet to page 2 and fold it back so that only page 2 shows. Assist the students if necessary. Then point to the box in the upper left corner of page 2.

Say, **"Busquen un cuadrito como éste en su página. Pongan su dedo en el cuadrito que tiene unas tijeras adentro".**

Check to see that each student has found the proper box. Then start reading the test items. *Do not read the item numbers.*

Say, **"Ahora quiten el dedo del cuadrito que tiene las tijeras adentro y tomen su lápiz".**

1. **"Miren los niños jugando en el resbaladero[1].** (Pause until you see that the students have found the correct picture.) **Encierren en un círculo el niño que está en lo *más alto.*** (Pause and observe the students.) **Encierren en un círculo el niño que está en lo *más alto".***

[1]Variation: *deslizadero, tobogán*

2. **"Miren las fresas que están en la bandeja.** (Pause until you see that the students have found the correct picture.) **Encierren en un círculo la fresa que está en *el centro* de la bandeja.** (Pause and observe the students.) **Encierren en un círculo la fresa que está en *el centro* de la bandeja".**
3. **"Miren las hamburguesas.** (Pause until you see that the students have found the correct picture.) **Encierren en un círculo el dibujo que muestra la hamburguesa *completa.*** (Pause and observe the students.) **Encierren en un círculo el dibujo que muestra la hamburguesa *completa".***
4. **"Miren los gatos y el sillón.** (Pause until you see that the students have found the correct picture.) **Encierren en un círculo el gato que está *al lado* del sillón.** (Pause and observe the students.) **Encierren en un círculo el gato que está *al lado* del sillón".**

Hold up your booklet and turn it so that page 3 shows. Tell the students, **"Pasen a la página siguiente".** Then point to the box on the upper right corner of page 3. Say, **"Ahora pongan su dedo en el cuadrito que tiene una pera adentro".** Make sure that everyone has found the correct page.

5. **"Miren los caballos.** (Pause until you see that the students have found the correct picture.) **Encierren en un círculo el *último* caballo de la fila.** (Pause and observe the students.) **Encierren en un círculo el *último* caballo de la fila".**
6. **"Miren los peces.** (Pause until you see that the students have found the correct picture.) **Encierren en un círculo el pez de tamaño *mediano.*** (Pause and observe the students.) **Encierren en un círculo el pez de tamaño *mediano".***
7. **"Miren el grifo, el timón, la perilla de puerta y el árbol.** (Pause until you see that the students have found the correct picture.) **Encierren en un circulo algo que *siempre* tiene un carro.** (Pause and observe the students.) **Encierren en un circulo algo que *siempre* tiene un carro".**
8. **"Miren los niños en la banqueta.** (Pause until you see that the students have found the correct picture.) **Encierren en un círculo el niño que está a la *derecha.*** (Pause and observe the students.) **Encierren en un círculo el niño que está a la *derecha".***

Turn your booklet to page 4 and fold it back. Tell the students, **"Pasen a la página siguiente".** Then point to the box on the upper left corner of page 4. Say, **"Ahora pongan su dedo en el cuadrito que tiene un foco[2] adentro".** Make sure that everyone has found the correct page.

9. **"Miren los ratoncitos.** (Pause until you see that the students have found the correct picture.) **Encierren en un círculo el ratoncito que está en la *esquina*[3] del cuarto.** (Pause and observe the students.) **Encierren en un círculo el ratoncito que está en la *esquina* del cuarto".**

---

[2] Variation: *bujia*

[3] Variation: *rincón*

10. **"Miren los dibujos de la camisa.** (Pause until you see that the students have found the correct picture.) **Encierren en un círculo el dibujo que muestra la camisa *antes* de ensuciarla.** (Pause and observe the students.) **Encierren en un círculo el dibujo que muestra la camisa *antes* de ensuciarla".**

11. **"Miren los perritos en la fila.** (Pause until you see that the students have found the correct picture.) **Encierren en un círculo el perrito que está al *final* de la fila.** (Pause and observe the students.) **Encierren en un círculo el perrito que está al *final* de la fila".**

12. **"Miren los pájaros y el árbol.** (Pause until you see that the students have found the correct picture.) **Encierren en un círculo el pájaro que está *más lejos* del árbol.** (Pause and observe the students.) **Encierren en un círculo el pájaro que está *más lejos* del árbol".**

Turn your booklet so that page 5 shows. Tell the students, **"Pasen a la página siguiente".** Then point to the box on the upper right corner of page 5. Say, **"Ahora pongan su dedo en el cuadrito que tiene una bicicleta adentro".** Make sure that everyone has found the correct page.

13. **"Miren los dibujos de las ranas.** (Pause until you see that the students have found the correct picture.) **Encierren en un círculo el dibujo que muestra sólo una *parte* de la rana.** (Pause and observe the students.) **Encierren en un círculo el dibujo que muestra sólo una *parte* de la rana".**

14. **"Miren los perritos.** (Pause until you see that the students have found the correct picture.) **Encierren en un círculo el perrito que está pasando *a través* del aro.** (Pause and observe the students.) **Encierren en un círculo el perrito que está pasando *a través* del aro".**

15. **"Miren el frasco con insectos.** (Pause until you see that the students have found the correct picture.) **Encierren en un círculo el frasco que tiene *algunos, pero no muchos* insectos.** (Pause and observe the students.) **Encierren en un círculo el frasco que tiene *algunos, pero no muchos* insectos".**

16. **"Miren los pájaros y el gato.** (Pause until you see that the students have found the correct picture.) **Encierren en un círculo el pájaro que está volando *arriba* del gato.** (Pause and observe the students.) **Encierren en un círculo el pájaro que está volando *arriba* del gato".**

Turn your booklet to page 6 and fold it back. Tell the students, **"Pasen a la página siguiente".** Then point to the box on the upper left corner of page 6. Say, **"Ahora pongan su dedo en el cuadrito que tiene un zapato adentro".** Make sure that everyone has found the correct page.

17. **"Miren los dibujos de las cuentas.** (Pause until you see that the students have found the correct picture.) **Encierren en un círculo el dibujo donde las cuentas están *separadas*.** (Pause and observe the students.) **Encierren en un círculo el dibujo donde las cuentas están *separadas*".**

18. **"Miren los estudiantes que están en la fila para almorzar.** (Pause until you see that the students have found the correct picture.) **Encierren en un círculo el *primer* niño de la fila.** (Pause and observe the students.) **Encierren en un círculo el *primer* niño de la fila".**

19. **"Miren los dibujos de los vasos.** (Pause until you see that the students have found the correct picture.) **Encierren en un círculo el dibujo donde todos los vasos están en *línea*.** (Pause and observe the students.) **Encierren en un círculo el dibujo donde todos los vasos están en *línea*".**

20. **"Miren los dibujos de los perritos.** (Pause until you see that the students have found the correct picture.) **Encierren en un círculo el dibujo que tiene *pocos* perritos.** (Pause and observe students.) **Encierren en un círculo el dibujo que tiene *pocos* perritos".**

Turn to page 7. Say, **"Pasen a la página siguiente. Ahora busquen el cuadrito que tiene un libro adentro".** Point to the box with the book in it. Make sure that everyone has found the correct page.

21. **"Miren la naranja, las uvas, la pera y la manzana.** (Pause until you see that the students have found the correct picture.) **Encierren en un círculo la fruta que está *más cerca* de la manzana.** (Pause and observe the students.) **Encierren en un círculo la fruta que está *más cerca* de la manzana".**

22. **"Miren los dibujos de los vasos y las cucharas.** (Pause until you see that the students have found the correct picture.) **Encierren en un círculo el dibujo que tiene una cuchara en *cada* vaso.** (Pause and observe the students.) **Encierren en un círculo el dibujo que tiene una cuchara en *cada* vaso".**

23. **"Miren los animales.** (Pause until you see that the students have found the correct picture.) **Encierren en un círculo el animal que está *más abajo*.** (Pause and observe the students.) **Encierren en un círculo el animal que está *más abajo*".**

24. **"Miren la camisa, el zapato, el vaso y el pantalón.** (Pause until you see that the students have found the correct picture.) **Encierren en un círculo el objeto que *nunca* se pone[4] un niño.** (Pause and observe the students.) **Encierren en un círculo el objeto que *nunca* se pone un niño".**

Turn to page 8. Say, **"Pasen a la página siguiente. Ahora busquen el cuadrito que tiene el sombrero adentro".** Point to the box with the hat in it. Make sure that everyone has found the correct page.

25. **"Miren los niños que están en el árbol.** (Pause until you see that the students have found the correct picture.) **Encierren en un círculo el niño que está *empezando* a subir al árbol.** (Pause and observe the students.) **Encierren en un círculo el niño que está *empezando* a subir al árbol".**

---

[4] Variation: *viste*

Note: If you are going to administer this test in *one* testing session, you may chose to skip the second set of practice items on page 9 of the test booklets.

If you have decided to administer this test in *two* testing sessions, you can stop testing here. When you continue testing, administer practice items *d, e,* and *f* before presenting items 26–50.

Turn to page 9. Say, **"Pasen a la página siguiente. Ahora busquen el cuadrito que tiene el helado[5] adentro".** Point to the box with the ice cream cone in it. Make sure that everyone has found the correct page.

Say, **"Ahora quiten el dedo del cuadrito que tiene el helado y tomen su lápiz".**

Wait until all the students have responded.

d. **"Miren el dibujo que tiene el zapato, la camisa, los pantalones y el calcetín.** (Show the students the correct place on the test booklet.) **Encierren en un círculo *la camisa.*** (Pause and observe students to make sure you have their attention before repeating the item.) **Encierren en un círculo *la camisa".***

Wait until all the students have responded. Make sure that all students have circled the shirt. Assist students who did not circle the shirt. Answer any questions.

e. **"Miren las cosas que se pueden montar.** (Show the students the correct place on the test booklet.) **Encierren en un círculo la *bicicleta.*** (Pause and observe the students.) **Encierren en un círculo la *bicicleta".***

Check the students' responses and assist those who did not circle the bicycle or who marked a picture other than the bicycle.

f. **"Miren las frutas.** (Show the students the correct place on the test booklet.) **Encierren en un círculo la *manzana.*** (Pause and observe the students.) **Encierren en un círculo la *manzana".***

Check the students' responses and assist those who did not circle the apple or who marked a picture other than the apple.

Then say, **"Si se equivocan o quieren cambiar una respuesta, táchenla con una X grande, así** (demonstrate on the chalkboard) **y después encierren en un círculo la nueva respuesta".**

When you see that everyone has marked his or her answers, say, **"Muy bien. Ahora dejen su lápiz en el escritorio. Voy a ver sus folletos. No vuelvan la página".**

This is your last opportunity to make sure that the students understand the task, as well as how to draw a circle on the form. Make certain that each student has circled the fork, the bird, and the chair. If anyone has marked the wrong answer, point out the error and have the student correct it. If any student has not clearly circled the fork, bird, or chair, show him or her how to do it.

---

[5] Variation: *sorbete, cono de nieve*

When all the work has been checked and the students appear confident that they understand what to do, start reading the test items.

Turn to page 10. Say, **"Pasen a la página siguiente. Ahora busquen el cuadrito que tiene un pescadito adentro".** Point to the box with the fish in it. Make sure that everyone has found the correct page.

26. **"Miren los animales y la puerta.** (Pause until you see that the students have found the correct picture.) **Encierren en un círculo el *segundo* animal, a partir de la puerta.** (Pause and observe the students.) **Encierren en un círculo el *segundo* animal, a partir de la puerta".**

27. **"Miren los patos y la niña.** (Pause until you see that the students have found the correct picture.) **Encierren en un círculo el pato que está *en frente* de la niña.** (Pause and observe the students.) **Encierren en un círculo el pato que está *en frente* de la niña".**

28. **"Miren las ventanas.** (Pause until you see that the students have found the correct picture.) **Encierren en un círculo la ventana *más ancha.*** (Pause and observe the students.) **Encierren en un círculo la ventana *más ancha".***

29. **"Miren los bloques y el bebé.** (Pause until you see that the students have found the correct picture.) **Encierren en un círculo el bloque que está *retirado* del bebé.** (Pause and observe the students.) **Encierren en un círculo el bloque que está *retirado* del bebé".**

Turn to page 11. Say, **"Pasen a la página siguiente. Ahora busquen el cuadrito que tiene un lápiz adentro".** Point to the box with the pencil in it. Make sure that everyone has found the correct page.

30. **"Miren los pasteles.**[6] (Pause until you see that the students have found the correct picture.) **Encierren en un círculo el dibujo que muestra la *mitad* de un pastel.** (Pause and observe the students.) **Encierren en un círculo el dibujo que muestra la *mitad* de un pastel".**

31. **"Miren los dibujos de los ositos de peluche.** (Pause until you see that the students have found the correct picture.) **Encierren en un círculo el dibujo donde los ositos son *iguales.*** (Pause and observe the students.) **Encierren en un círculo el dibujo donde los ositos son *iguales".***

32. **"Miren los dibujos de las estrellas.** (Pause until you see that the students have found the correct picture.) **Encierren en un círculo el dibujo que tiene *la menor cantidad* de estrellas.** (Pause and observe the students.) **Encierren en un círculo el dibujo que tiene *la menor cantidad* de estrellas".**

[6] Variation: *tortas, pan dulce, postres*

33. **"Miren los dibujos de la ropa.** (Pause until you see that the students have found the correct picture.) **Encierren en un círculo el dibujo donde la ropa *hace juego".*[7]** (Pause and observe the students.) **Encierren en un círculo el dibujo donde la ropa *hace juego".***

Turn to page 12. Say, **"Pasen a la página siguiente. Ahora busquen el cuadrito que tiene una pluma adentro".** Point to the box with the feather in it. Make sure that everyone has found the correct page.

34. **"Miren los niños y la cuerda.** (Pause until you see that the students have found the correct picture.) **Encierren en un círculo el niño que está saltando *sobre* la cuerda.** (Pause and observe the students.) **Encierren en un círculo el niño que está saltando *sobre* la cuerda".**

35. **"Miren los lápices que están en la gaveta.** (Point to the drawer. Pause until you see that the students have found the correct picture.) **Encierren en un círculo el dibujo que tiene *tantos* lápices *como* hay en la gaveta.** (Pause and observe the students.) **Encierren en un círculo el dibujo que tiene *tantos* lápices *como* hay en la gaveta".**

36. **"Miren el árbol y las casas.** (Pause until you see that the students have found the correct picture.) **Encierren en un círculo la *tercera* casa a partir del árbol.** (Pause and observe the students.) **Encierren en un círculo la *tercera* casa a partir del árbol".**

37. **"Miren los animales. Uno es un cerdo[8] y otro es un conejo.** (Pause until you see that the students have found the correct picture.) **Encierren en un círculo el *otro* animal.** (Pause and observe the students.) **Encierren en un círculo el *otro* animal".**

Turn to page 13. Say, **"Pasen a la página siguiente. Ahora busquen el cuadrito que tiene una cuchara adentro".** Point to the box with the spoon in it. Make sure that everyone has found the correct page.

38. **"Miren los dibujos de la niña que va a pescar.** (Pause until you see that the students have found the correct picture.) **Encierren en un círculo el dibujo donde la niña está *empezando* a pescar.** (Pause and observe the students.) **Encierren en un círculo el dibujo donde la niña está *empezando* a pescar".**

39. **"Miren las cajas con botones.** (Pause until you see that the students have found the correct picture.) **Encierren en un círculo la caja que tiene *más* botones.** (Pause and observe the students.) **Encierren en un círculo la caja que tiene *más* botones".**

[7] Variation: *hacen pareja*

[8] Variation: *chancho, marrano, puerco, cochino*

40. **"Miren el matorral[9] y los niños.** (Pause until you see that the students have found the correct picture.) **Encierren en un círculo el niño que está *detrás* del matorral.** (Pause and observe students.) **Encierren en un círculo el niño que está *detrás* del matorral".**

41. **"Miren los ratoncitos.** (Pause until you see that the students have found the correct picture.) **Encierren en un círculo el ratoncito que está a la *izquierda.*** (Pause and observe the students.) **Encierren en un círculo el ratoncito que está a la *izquierda".***

Turn to page 14. Say, **"Pasen a la página siguiente. Ahora busquen el cuadrito que tiene una mariposa adentro".** Point to the box with the butterfly in it. Make sure that everyone has found the correct page.

42. **"Miren los dibujos de los bloques y los ositos.** (Pause until you see that the students have found the correct picture.) **Encierren en un círculo el dibujo que tiene un osito *en medio de* dos bloques.** (Pause and observe the students.) **Encierren en un círculo el dibujo que tiene un osito *en medio de* dos bloques".**

43. **"Miren los gatos.** (Pause until you see that the students have found the correct picture.) **Encierren en un círculo el gato que es *diferente.*** (Pause and observe the students.) **Encierren en un círculo el gato que es *diferente".***

44. **"Miren los dibujos de los guantes.** (Pause until you see that the students have found the correct picture.) **Encierren en un círculo el dibujo que muestra un *par* de guantes.** (Pause and observe the students.) **Encierren en un círculo el dibujo que muestra un *par* de guantes".**

45. **"Miren las arañas.** (Pause until you see that the students have found the correct picture.) **Encierren en un círculo la araña que está *debajo* del anaquel.**[10] (Pause and observe the students.) **Encierren en un círculo la araña que está *debajo* del anaquel".**

Turn to page 15. Say, **"Pasen a la página siguiente. Ahora busquen el cuadrito que tiene una flor adentro".** Point to the box with the flower in it. Make sure that everyone has found the correct page.

46. **"Encuentren el círculo que tiene una estrella adentro.** (Pause until you see that the students have found the correct picture.) ***Sáltense* una estrella y hagan un círculo en la siguiente estrella.** (Pause and observe the students.) **Encuentren el círculo que tiene una estrella adentro. *Sáltense* una estrella y hagan un círculo en la siguiente estrella".**

47. **"Miren los dibujos del niño.** (Pause until you see that the students have found the correct picture.) **Encierren en un círculo el dibujo donde el niño está *inclinado* hacia adelante.** (Pause and observe the students.) **Encierren en un círculo el dibujo donde el niño está *inclinado* hacia adelante".**

[9] Variation: *la mata*

[10] Variation: *estante*

48. **"Miren los platos de fideos.** (Pause until you see that the students have found the correct picture.) **Encierren en un círculo el plato que tiene *menos* fideos.** (Pause and observe the students.) **Encierren en un círculo el plato que tiene *menos* fideos".**

49. **"Miren la rana que está en el cuadrito.** (Point to the frog in the box. Pause until you see that the students have found the correct picture.) **Hagan un círculo en el cuadrito donde quedará la rana después de haber saltado un espacio *hacia atrás.*** (Pause and observe the students.) **Hagan un círculo en el cuadrito donde quedará la rana después de haber saltado un espacio *hacia atrás".***

Turn to page 16. Say, **"Pasen a la página siguiente. Ahora busquen el cuadrito que tiene un teléfono adentro".** Point to the box with the telephone in it. Make sure that everyone has found the correct page.

50. **"Miren estas manos con dulces.** (Pause until you see that the students have found the correct picture.) **Encierren en un círculo las manos que tienen *igual* número de dulces.** (Pause and observe the students.) **Encierren en un círculo las manos que tienen *igual* número de dulces".**

When students have completed item 50, say, **"Ya terminamos. Dejen sus lápices sobre el escritorio. Cierren sus folletos y yo los voy a recoger".**

Scoring and Recording the Results

There are three key forms to enable you to score and record Boehm–3 results for each student in your classroom. They are the *Class Record Form and Scoring Key*, the *Test Summary and Teacher Observation Form*, and the *Parent Report Form*. By using all three of these forms with the student's test booklet, you can establish a complete profile and instructional plan.

Completing the Class Record Form and Scoring Key

The *Class Record Form and Scoring Key* provides a convenient way to score students' test booklets and record test results for an entire classroom. The *Class Record Form* serves both as a scoring key and as an interpretive aid. It is designed to speed recording of students' scores and facilitate analysis of their test results. If there are more than 30 students in the class, fasten two *Class Record Forms* together so that the entries in the shaded column headed "Total Number of Students Answering Correctly" and the adjacent column headed "Percent Passing" will be based on the scores of the entire class.

The concepts tested are listed in item order down the left-hand side of the form. Each concept is accompanied by a miniature reproduction of the picture with which it is tested. The correct response is circled. Use this miniature key to score the students' test booklets. Alternatively, you can mark a set of test booklets with the correct answers and use them as scoring keys.

Across the top of the *Class Record Form* are spaces for entering the names of the students tested. Write the students' names at the top of the form in the spaces provided. Beginning with item 1, compare the student's response to the scoring key. Place a *1* for a correct response in the box corresponding to item 1. If the student's response was incorrect, leave the space blank or you may code it with *NR* for no response, *A* for antonym or the opposite of the target concept, *E* if every response was marked, or *M* for miscellaneous/other. See the Optional Error Analysis section on page 54 in this manual for further explanation. Follow the same procedure for each of the remaining items. See Figure 2.1 for an example. Be careful to record the score in the correct column for each student. This sometimes poses a problem for the items that occur later in the test because of the distance between the student's name and the item boxes. It may be helpful to fold the *Class Record Form* back along the line between items 25 and 26, and to place this fold along the line immediately above item 1, leaving only the boxes for items 26 through 50 exposed.

CONCEPTS		1 Maria Cerda	2 John Phillips	3 Jennifer James	4 Shawna Brown	5 Ashley Hodson	6 Michael Lee	7 Chris Thompson	8 Raymond Lozano	9 Jeremy Duncan	10 Kelly Hoffman	11 Julie Martinez	12 Amy Chan	13 Paul Rodriguez	14 Kaycie Willard	15 Madison Goldstein
1. Top Más alto		1	1	1	1	1	1	1	1	1	1	1	1	1	E	1
2. Center El centro	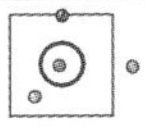	1	NR	M	1	1	1	1	M	1	M	1	1	1	1	1
3. Whole Completo	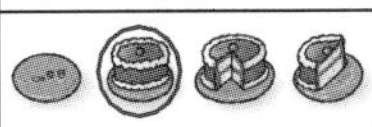	1	1	1	A	1	A	1	1	NR	1	1	1	A	1	A
4. Side Al lado		1	1	1	1	1	E	1	1	1	1	1	1	1	1	1
5. Last Último		1	1	1	1	1	1	1	1	A	1	1	1	1	1	1
6. Medium-sized Mediano		M	1	1	E	1	1	1	1	1	1	1	1	1	E	1

Figure 2.1 Example of a *Class Record Form* With Scores in Correct Boxes

Once you've counted and entered the scores for all items for all students, total the number of items that each student answered correctly. Enter this total in the appropriate place in the shaded row labeled "Raw Score" at the bottom of the form. Then for each item, count the number of students who answered correctly and write this number in the column labeled "Total Number of Students Answering Correctly" at the right side of the form. To determine the percent of students who answered each item correctly, look at Appendix A in the *Examiner's Manual.* Complete instructions are included in that table. Enter these percents in the column at the right, labeled "Percent Passing." See Figure 2.2 for an example.

STUDENT'S NAME

CONCEPTS		1 Maria Cerda	2 John Phillips	3 Jennifer James	4 Shawna Brown	5 Ashley Hodson	6 Michael Lee	7 Chris Thompson	8 Raymond Lozano	9 Jeremy Duncan	10 Kelly Hoffman	11 Julie Martinez	12 Amy Chan	13 Paul Rodriguez	14 Kaycie Willard	15 Madison Goldstein	16	17	18	19	20	21	22	23	24	25	26	27	28	29	30	TOTAL NUMBER OF STUDENTS ANSWERING CORRECTLY	PERCENT PASSING ✓ % = Number answering correctly / Number tested x 100
1. Top Más alto		I	I	I	I	I	I	I	I	I	I	I	I	I	E	I																14	93
2. Center El centro		I	NR	M	I	I	I	I	M	I	M	I	I	I	I	I																11	73
3. Whole Completo		I	I	I	A	I	A	I	I	NR	I	I	I	A	I	A																10	67
4. Side Al lado		I	I	I	I	I	E	I	I	I	I	I	I	I	I	I																14	93
5. Last Último		I	I	I	I	I	I	I	I	A	I	I	I	I	I	I																14	93
6. Medium-sized Mediano		M	I	I	E	I	I	I	I	I	I	I	I	I	E	I																12	80

Figure 2.2 Example of Percent Passing as Recorded in the *Class Record Form*

Add the numbers in the row labeled "Raw Score" and write the total in the space labeled "Sum." (This number should match the sum of the column titled "Total Number of Students Answering Correctly." If it doesn't, the totals are not the same. Check for counting errors before proceeding.) Divide the sum by the total number of students tested and record the number in the box labeled "Class Average." This is the class average raw score.

You can convert the student's raw score (Total Number of Items Answered Correctly) to percent correct by looking at the table in this manual on page 96. Record the percent correct in the appropriate row under raw score. To determine the performance range, locate the appropriate table (4.22 or 4.23) by language, grade, form, and time of testing on page 97. You must use the student's raw score to find the appropriate performance range. Record the range number on the *Class Record Form* in the row titled "Performance Range." If you choose to report a corresponding percentile, look at tables 4.24 and 4.25 on pages 98–99. Locate the appropriate table by form. Use the student's raw score, grade, and time of testing to determine the percentile. See pages 121–124 for the Spanish edition normative data.

When you've completed the *Class Record Form*, it may be helpful to fold the form just above the "Raw Score" and "Percent Correct" rows, then align this with the bottom of the "Student's Name" section. This will facilitate reading each student's scores.

Optional Error Analysis

Many errors young students make are systematic and therefore useful to the teacher when planning instruction. You may wish to record errors, as well as correct responses, on the *Class Record Form*. This may be accomplished simply by using a red pencil and entering the following codes in the appropriate column when an error has been made.

This information may be summed for a particular student and for the entire class.

Code	Type of Error
NR	No response
A	Antonym or opposite of the target concept was chosen, such as *top* instead of *bottom*
E	Every picture (or every component of the pictured item) was marked
M	Miscellaneous—response suggests another explanation for error

Completing the *Test Summary and Teacher Observation Form* for Each Student

This form was developed to assist you or the interventionist in instructional planning. Complete the information about the student. The *Test Summary* provides a recap of the student's performance on the test overall and on each item. In the student's *Test Summary,* place an X by any concept the student missed during the recent test administration. You can complete this summary at the beginning and end of the school year, or before and after intervention. Use a different color for each observation date to make it easy to see the changes that occur across time.

Proceed to the section called *Teacher Observations of Basic Concepts Used Across Curriculum Areas*, where you can record observations of the student's use of basic concepts across contexts, over time.

Observations are organized into four curriculum areas, including concepts that are essential for

1. following teacher directions and classroom activities, including primarily spatial or positional concepts;
2. reading, including primarily temporal concepts;
3. mathematics and science, including primarily quantitative and size concepts; and
4. general, including concepts that occur in all curriculum areas.

A student's understanding of basic concepts in one context does not ensure understanding in another. The teacher's observations of a student's use of concepts across contexts is essential for instructional planning.

The final section of this form focuses on using concepts as thinking tools. Record observations and examples of a student's use of concepts for a variety of problem-solving situations. For example, students need to

- follow directions that include more than one concept,
- follow directions that include more than one step,
- use concepts to make comparative judgements,
- use concepts to make comparisons to a standard,
- use basic concepts for ordering,
- use basic concepts to group or classify by one or more characteristics,
- use basic concepts to solve problems at increasing levels of difficulty, and
- use basic concepts not in order of mention (e.g., You may get your snack after you wash your hands).

The *Test Summary and Teacher Observation Form* (English) is designed for use with *Form E* and *Form F* and is located at the back of each test booklet. The reproducible Spanish version of the *Test Summary and Teacher Observation Form* can be found on page 43 in the *Directions for Administration (English and Spanish, Forms* E and *F)* component.

Figure 2.3 is an example of the completed *Test Summary and Teacher Observation Form*. This form can be helpful for developing and/or adjusting objectives and for reporting progress. The *Test Summary and Teacher Observation Form* can easily be removed from the student's test booklet and added to the cumulative record. For activities that encourage students to use basic concepts in a variety of curriculum contexts and for teaching ideas, refer to the intervention section of this manual and the *Boehm Resource Guide for Basic Concept Teaching* (Boehm, 1976).

Boehm·3
Boehm Test of Basic Concepts · Third Edition

Test Summary and Teacher Observation Form

Child's Name Julie Martinez Age 6 Grade K

Teacher/Evaluator Mr. Thompson School Lincoln Elementary

Language the child speaks at home English

Date Tested 10/13 (Form E) Form F Raw Score 45 % Correct 90 Performance Range 1 Percentile 80

Date Tested ______ Form E Form F Raw Score ____ % Correct ____ Performance Range ____ Percentile ____

—— *Child's Performance Summary* ——

Place an X in the blank next to the number of the item missed. Use this form for more than one administration by using a different color of ink each time. (**Space** *Where* = Red; **Quantity** *How many?* = Green; **Time** *When* = Blue; **Other** = Orange)

Item	Concept	Item	Concept	Item	Concept
	1. Top		18. First		35. As Many
	2. Center		19. Row		36. Third
	3. Whole		20. Few		37. Other
	4. Side		21. Next		38. Starting
	5. Last		22. Every		39. Most
	6. Medium-sized		23. Bottom		40. Behind
	7. Always		24. Never		41. Left
	8. Right		25. Beginning		42. Between
	9. Corner		26. Second		43. Different
	10. Before		27. Front		44. Pair
	11. End		28. Widest		45. Below
	12. Farthest		29. Away	X	46. Skip
	13. Part		30. Half		47. Forward
	14. Through		31. Alike		48. Least
	15. Some	X	32. Fewest	X	49. Backward
	16. Above		33. Match	X	50. Equal
X	17. Separated		34. Over		

Teacher Observations of Basic Concepts Used Across Curriculum Areas

Curriculum Area	Concept	Observed	Comments/Examples
Following teacher directions and classroom activities	*top*–bottom**		
	over–*under**		
	*next to**		
	through		
	first–last**		
	above-below		
	corner		
	side		
	in front of—behind		
	*away from**		
	nearest–farthest**		
	separated		
	alike (*same*)–*different**		
	match		
	left–right		
	center		
	forward–(backward)	11/15	Used the concept "backward" during storytime.
	always–never		
	(skip)	12/3	Demonstrated understanding of skip by skipping lines on her paper when directed to.
	every		
	row		
	*between**		
	beginning–end		
	other		

Figure 2.3 Example of a Completed *Test Summary and Teacher Observation Form*

Completing the *Parent Report Form*

The *Parent Report Form* is located on the last page of the test booklet. It is designed to aid teachers in presenting Boehm–3 test results to parents. A reproducible Spanish translation of this form can be found on page 45 of the *Directions for Administration*. The *Parent Report Form* includes an explanation of basic concepts, a brief description of the test, a sample test item, student test results, a list of concepts that were tested, and suggestions for parents to help their students learn basic concepts in and around the home. This form may aid parents in understanding their role as partners with teachers—a joint effort to help students be successful in school.

Fill in the student's name and date of testing at the top of the form. In the Test Results section, enter the number of items the student identified correctly out of 50. This is the raw score. Then, refer to the performance range already recorded on the *Class Record Form* or to Tables 4.22 or 4.23 on page 97 that lists performance ranges by grade and form for the English edition. This information for students who were administered the Spanish edition can be found on page 122. Using the student's raw score, determine whether the student's performance range is a 1, 2, or 3. Circle the corresponding number under Performance Range on the *Parent Report Form.* Beside each number is a description of the student's performance in relation to his or her grade-level peers. Locate the list of concepts tested with Boehm–3. Circle the concepts that the student missed.

The *Parent Report* also includes suggestions for ways in which the parent or caregiver can help their child learn basic concepts at home. You can make comments in the Teacher's Notes section provided or target particular concepts or activities to be worked on at home and sign the form. Detach the *Parent Report Form* from the test booklet to send it home with the student or share it with the parents or caregivers in a conference. Figure 2.4 is an example of a completed *Parent Report Form.*

Boehm·3
Boehm Test of Basic Concepts · Third Edition

Parent Report

Child's Name Kelly Hoffman Date of Testing 11/6

Your child recently took the *Boehm Test of Basic Concepts–3*, a test designed to measure your child's knowledge of basic concepts. The *Boehm–3* measures understanding of basic concepts including those related to **space** (*above, below*), **quantity** (*medium-sized, few*), and **time** (*before, beginning,*) and a few others. Knowledge of these concepts is necessary for

- **following teachers' verbal instructions (*Open* your book to the *first* page.)**
- **developing reading skills (Find *all* the words that *begin* with the letter *s*.)**
- **learning math skills (Which group has *more* apples?)**
- **engaging in activities that involve reasoning (Put *all* the baby animals *together*.) and**
- **communicating more precisely to others (I would like the *first* book on the *top* shelf.)**

The following is an example of one of the test items. Your child would be asked to "circle the balloon that is over the fence."

Test Results

By the end of the first grade, most children should know all or almost all of the basic concepts. The test results indicate the concepts your child knows and the concepts he or she needs to learn. Your child answered 46 /50 items correctly. Look at the performance ranges and the explanation that follows. I have circled the performance range for your child's score. The explanation will tell you how well your child understands basic concepts.

Performance Range	Explantion
1	Student knows the basic concepts needed to perform at his or her grade level.
(2)	Student knows most of the basic concepts needed to perform at his or her grade level, but lacks understanding of some key concepts.
3	Student's knowledge of basic concepts is extremely low for his/her grade. Teacher and parent help is needed for the child's success in school.

These basic concepts were included in the test. Your child needs practice with the concepts that are circled. You can check these results with what you see your child do at home. Give your child plenty of opportunities to use the concepts he or she knows, too. The goal is for your child to be able to use all of these concepts in many different situations.

Concepts Tested with Boehm–3

1. Top	11. End	21. Next	31. Alike	(41. Left)
2. Center	12. Farthest	22. Every	(32. Fewest)	42. Between
3. Whole	13. Part	23. Bottom	33. Match	43. Different
4. Side	14. Through	24. Never	34. Over	44. Pair
5. Last	(15. Some)	25. Beginning	35. As Many	45. Below
6. Medium-sized	16. Above	26. Second	36. Third	(46. Skip)
7. Always	17. Separated	27. Front	37. Other	47. Forward
8. Right	18. First	28. Widest	38. Starting	48. Least
9. Corner	19. Row	29. Away	39. Most	49. Backward
10. Before	20. Few	30. Half	40. Behind	50. Equal

Space *Where* = Red **Quantity** *How many?* = Green **Time** *When* = Blue **Other** = Orange

Figure 2.4 Example of a *Completed Parent Report Form*

Chapter 3
Planning Intervention

Using the Test Results

How you plan to use Boehm–3 results will partly determine how you interpret those results. Because the questions of use and interpretation are so closely interrelated, it is necessary to discuss them together.

The first step in interpretation is to identify those students with particularly low scores who may have difficulty with concept learning and need special help. However, in deciding whether or not a score is to be regarded as "undesirably low," keep the student's first language in mind. Consider a student's first or home language if he or she performs poorly on the test when it is administered in English. The next step is to determine whether the student knows the missed concepts in his or her first language. The interpretation of this student's overall score also needs to be reconsidered and is likely to be higher.

It is also important to remember that students at the kindergarten level scoring at the 50th percentile still have many basic concepts to learn. This is particularly true for the beginning of the school year or fall testing. Kindergarten may be the student's first exposure to some of the basic concepts presented in Boehm–3. If this is the case, you may use the results of the fall testing for instructional planning and test the student again in the spring to determine his or her progress.

Review the students' scores located at the bottom of the *Class Record Form*. An explanation of each type of score follows the example given in Figure 3.1.

Hacia atrás																
50. Equal / Igual	I	I	I	I	I	M	I	I	I	I	M	I	M	I	NR	11 / 73
RAW SCORE	39	47	50	43	50	48	46	50	49	42	38	45	40	46	41	Sum☆ 674 / Class Avg.† 44.9
PERCENT CORRECT	78	94	100	86	100	96	92	100	98	84	76	90	80	92	82	TOTAL NUMBER OF STUDENTS TESTED
PERFORMANCE RANGE	2	1	1	2	1	1	1	1	1	2	2	1	2	1	2	
PERCENTILE	43	92	99	65	99	96	87	99	98	58	38	80	47	87	53	N= 15

✓ See Appendix A in the *Examiner's Manual* for the Percent Passing Table.

☆ Sum of shaded row should equal sum of shaded column. If not, check for error. †Class Average = Sum / Number tested

PERFORMANCE RANGE	EXPLANATION
1	Student knows the basic concepts needed to perform at his or her grade level.
2	Student knows most of the basic concepts needed to perform at his or her grade level, but lacks understanding of some key concepts.
3	Student's knowledge of basic concepts is extremely low for his/her grade. Teacher and parent help is needed for the student's success in school.

CODE	TYPE OF ERROR
NR	No Response
A	Antonym or opposite of the target concept was chosen, such as ***top*** instead of ***bottom***
E	Every picture was marked
M	Miscellaneous—response suggests another explanation for error

Figure 3.1 Example of the Score Section of a *Class Record Form*

The first row contains the *raw score*. Simply stated, it is the total number of items the student identified correctly. You may have a goal or expectation for your class. For example, "All kindergarten students should know 35 out of 50 concepts at the beginning of the year to be successful in the classroom." Students who answer very few items correctly will probably benefit from special instruction in the concepts missed (regardless of how well or poorly other students performed on the test) because the concepts are basic to understanding and following classroom directions. Whether or not a student should be singled out for individual attention depends upon the overall performance of the class. The class average is located in the lower right corner of the *Class Record Form*. If the class average on the test is low, the class as a whole is likely to benefit from instruction and embedded emphasis on basic concepts within the context of natural, ongoing, classroom activities. On the other hand, if the class average is high, you need to ensure that basic concept use is generalized across contexts, giving special attention to the concepts that are occasionally missed by a large proportion of the class. Individual attention is needed only for those students who perform poorly. One way of selecting such students would be to identify the students whose scores lie below the class average. Because basic concepts are an important aspect of language, you may want to consult with the speech-language pathologist early on about these students.

The second row contains the *percent correct*. This score indicates the percentage out of 100 that the student answered correctly. You may have chosen a percent correct criteria for your class. For example, "All students should achieve 75% correct at the beginning of school." It is important to remember that at the end of first grade, most students should know most of the concepts tested by the Boehm–3.

The third row contains the *performance range*. This score is indicated by a 1, 2, or 3. A student performing in the first (1) range knows the concepts needed to perform at his or her grade level. A student performing in the second (2) range knows most of the concepts needed to perform at his or her grade level, but may lack understanding of some key basic concepts. A student performing in the third (3) range has a low level of knowledge of basic concepts when compared to others in his or her same grade. This child will definitely need some additional help from teachers, parents and/or others to be successful in school.

The fourth and final row contains the *percentile*. This score can be described as "The student is performing as well as or better than ___% of the class." This score can be confusing. You may notice that a second-grade student who misses only 1 item on a fall administration of the English version of the test has a percentile score of 67. This does not necessarily mean that the student is a candidate for individual or specialized services. It is possible that during the presentation of an item, the student may have been inattentive. You may want to administer this item at a later time to check on the student's understanding of the concept. It is particularly important to note that many second-grade students (over 40%) in the fall standardization sample demonstrated understanding of all 50 concepts. Missing one or two items greatly reduces the percentile score.

To summarize, the teacher should base any choice of intervention upon three considerations:

- the average performance of the class as a whole, and
- the individual performance of specific students.
- the student's home language

When most of the students in the class obtain low scores, small group training procedures are recommended, as well as embedding the missed concepts in ongoing classroom activities. When the group as a whole performs well, special instruction for individual students is desirable.

The Boehm–3 was developed to help teachers assess a student's knowledge of important concepts in simple forms. None of the items require the student to distinguish between comparatives and superlatives, such as "bigger than one, but not the biggest." Similarly, no item attempts to assess whether the student can make other important applications of concepts, such as knowing that the *top* of a ladder becomes its *bottom* if the ladder is turned upside down, or that Jared's box of pencils has *more* pencils than Steven's, but *less* than José's.

The items in *Forms E* and *F* are presented in a relatively simple form because the concepts they embody are most often used the same way in the "Directions" portions of curriculum materials. Many concepts, however, are used in combination in curriculum materials. For example, students may be asked to identify *all* of the words that *end* with the *same* sound. For the same reason, instructional activities should start with a presentation of the concepts in a concrete, simple form before more complex uses are presented. This will help ensure that students with poorer concept knowledge assimilate the simplest meanings of the concepts necessary for understanding instruction. It is particularly important that you model basic concept terms frequently during their daily activities. You might also review the complexity of your verbal directions and the number of steps needed for students to comply with instruction and classroom activities.

Selecting Concepts for Instruction

You should begin planning your classroom instructions by identifying the concepts missed or omitted by a large number of students. Any concept understood by less than 100% of the students in a class should, ideally, be considered a target for intervention. By the end of first grade, most students, with the exception of those presenting special learning needs, should know all or almost all of the concepts.

Be practical about the number of concepts you can cover in class activities. You may not want to focus on more than 10 to 15 concepts during a 2- to 3-month period. Use Tables 3.1 and 3.2 for a description of the concepts by type (e.g., spatial [location, direction, orientation, dimensions], quantitative [number], temporal [time], and other) and level of difficulty to determine appropriate concepts or concept progression for students who were administered Boehm–3 in English. This information was compiled by looking at the number of students passing the item from the overall English standardization groups. Use Table 3.1 for fall or Table 3.2 for spring testing. For students who were administered Boehm–3 in Spanish, see Tables 3.3 or 3.4. This information was compiled by looking at the number of students passing the item from the Spanish standardization group. You can also use information about the percentage of various groups passing each item by form (reported in chapter 4 [English] and chapter 5 [Spanish]) to help you select concepts for instruction. See Appendices E (English) and F (Spanish) for concepts listed from least to most difficult by grade.

Several concepts that were administered to students in Spanish did not follow a typical progression. It is possible that in English these concepts are more concrete, while in Spanish, the concept is relative to the proximity of a person or location. For example, *next* in Spanish relates to the closeness or proximity of one object or person to another. While this is true in some contexts in English, it is not universally. In addition, some concepts in Spanish may have more than one meaning. For example, the word *sobre* in Spanish can reflect both the prepositions *over* and *on*.

Reviewing the Errors Students Make to Guide Instructional Planning

Many of the errors students make are part of a pattern and can be useful when considering instructional strategies. Past reviews of errors by researchers studying concept development suggest that a student's responses are related to his or her age, past experience, and level of cognitive development (Blewitt, 1982; Clark, 1983). The errors students make can help teachers raise hypotheses about the reasons for these errors. These hypotheses can then be investigated by observation, a strategy interview, and by tasks developed to target each problem. For example, the student who marks the antonym of the basic concept targeted by an item may know something about the concept dimension and, therefore, instruction probably does not need to start from scratch. Rather, instruction can help the student focus on differentiating the opposite terms through the presentation of examples and non-examples of the concept. If this pattern exists for other students as well, the teacher has gained important information for instruction. The summary of errors on the *Class Record Form* has been added to help focus attention on the types of errors made. As another example, the student who does not respond to many items may not know the concepts involved, may be unfamiliar with the concept label, or may not have paid attention. Whatever the reason, the teacher should try to determine the nature of the error. It is also important to follow up the results of the test through observation as students are engaged in everyday classroom activities.

The Boehm–3 is used to assess concepts applied in one context that can be depicted through pictures. However, many concepts are applied in more than one context, and each context needs to be considered for instruction. For example, the concepts *first* and *last* are used to describe positions in space, time, and number series. The student's ability to use the concept to describe spatial positions does not insure his or her understanding of how the concept is used to describe story sequences. As another example, the concepts *alike* and *different* can be used to describe relationships involving space, quantity, time, taste, smell, behaviors, and feelings. The classification of concepts into four types, summarized in Tables 3.1 through 3.4, are arbitrary to some extent and other meaningful classifications could be suggested. These concepts are further

TABLE 3.1 Concepts by Type and Level of Difficulty—Fall Testing

Item No.	Concept	Type of Concept	Level of Difficulty Kindergarten	1st Grade	2nd Grade
1	Top	Spatial	Very easy	Very easy	Very easy
2	Center	Spatial	Easy	Very easy	Very easy
3	Whole	Quantitative	Very easy	Very easy	Very easy
4	Side	Spatial	Easy	Very easy	Very easy
5	Last	Spatial	Easy	Very easy	Very easy
6	Medium-sized	Quantitative	Difficult	Easy	Very easy
7	Always	Temporal	Very easy	Very easy	Very easy
8	Right	Spatial	Difficult	Easy	Easy
9	Corner	Spatial	Easy	Very easy	Very easy
10	Before	Temporal	Difficult	Easy	Very easy
11	End	Spatial	Easy	Very easy	Very easy
12	Farthest	Spatial	Very easy	Very easy	Very easy
13	Part	Quantitative	Easy	Very easy	Very easy
14	Through	Spatial	Very easy	Very easy	Very easy
15	Some	Quantitative	Difficult	Difficult	Easy
16	Above	Spatial	Easy	Very easy	Very easy
17	Separated	Spatial	Difficult	Easy	Very easy
18	First	Quantitative	Very easy	Very easy	Very easy
19	Row	Spatial	Very easy	Very easy	Very easy
20	Few	Quantitative	Very easy	Very easy	Very easy
21	Next	Spatial	Easy	Very easy	Very easy
22	Every	Quantitative	Difficult	Easy	Easy
23	Bottom	Spatial	Easy	Very easy	Very easy
24	Never	Temporal	Difficult	Very easy	Very easy
25	Beginning	Temporal	Difficult	Easy	Very easy
26	Second	Quantitative	Difficult	Very easy	Very easy
27	Front	Spatial	Very easy	Very easy	Very easy
28	Widest	Quantitative	Easy	Easy	Very easy
29	Away	Spatial	Very easy	Very easy	Very easy
30	Half	Quantitative	Easy	Very easy	Very easy
31	Alike	Spatial	Easy	Very easy	Very easy
32	Fewest	Quantitative	Very difficult	Difficult	Difficult
33	Match	Other	Very easy	Very easy	Very easy
34	Over	Spatial	Very easy	Very easy	Very easy
35	As Many	Quantitative	Easy	Very easy	Very easy
36	Third	Quantitative	Difficult	Very easy	Very easy
37	Other	Other	Difficult	Easy	Very easy
38	Starting	Temporal	Easy	Very easy	Very easy
39	Most	Quantitative	Easy	Very easy	Very easy
40	Behind	Spatial	Easy	Very easy	Very easy
41	Left	Spatial	Difficult	Difficult	Easy
42	Between	Spatial	Easy	Easy	Very easy
43	Different	Quantitative	Easy	Very easy	Very easy
44	Pair	Quantitative	Easy	Very easy	Very easy
45	Below	Spatial	Easy	Very easy	Very easy
46	Skip	Spatial	Very difficult	Difficult	Easy
47	Forward	Spatial	Difficult	Easy	Very easy
48	Least	Quantitative	Difficult	Easy	Very easy
49	Backward	Spatial	Difficult	Easy	Very easy
50	Equal	Quantitative	Very difficult	Easy	Very easy

TABLE 3.2 Concepts by Type and Level of Difficulty—Spring Testing

Item No.	Concept	Type of Concept	Level of Difficulty Kindergarten	1st Grade	2nd Grade
1	Top	Spatial	Very easy	Very easy	Very easy
2	Center	Spatial	Easy	Very easy	Very easy
3	Whole	Quantitative	Very easy	Very easy	Very easy
4	Side	Spatial	Very easy	Very easy	Very easy
5	Last	Spatial	Very easy	Very easy	Very easy
6	Medium-sized	Quantitative	Easy	Very easy	Very easy
7	Always	Temporal	Very easy	Very easy	Very easy
8	Right	Spatial	Difficult	Easy	Easy
9	Corner	Spatial	Very easy	Very easy	Very easy
10	Before	Temporal	Easy	Easy	Very easy
11	End	Spatial	Very easy	Very easy	Very easy
12	Farthest	Spatial	Very easy	Very easy	Very easy
13	Part	Quantitative	Very easy	Very easy	Very easy
14	Through	Spatial	Very easy	Very easy	Very easy
15	Some	Quantitative	Easy	Easy	Very easy
16	Above	Spatial	Very easy	Very easy	Very easy
17	Separated	Spatial	Easy	Easy	Very easy
18	First	Quantitative	Very easy	Very easy	Very easy
19	Row	Spatial	Very easy	Very easy	Very easy
20	Few	Quantitative	Very easy	Very easy	Very easy
21	Next	Spatial	Easy	Easy	Very easy
22	Every	Quantitative	Very easy	Very easy	Very easy
23	Bottom	Spatial	Very easy	Very easy	Very easy
24	Never	Temporal	Easy	Very easy	Very easy
25	Beginning	Temporal	Very easy	Very easy	Very easy
26	Second	Quantitative	Easy	Very easy	Very easy
27	Front	Spatial	Very easy	Very easy	Very easy
28	Widest	Quantitative	Easy	Very easy	Very easy
29	Away	Spatial	Very easy	Very easy	Very easy
30	Half	Quantitative	Easy	Very easy	Very easy
31	Alike	Spatial	Very easy	Very easy	Very easy
32	Fewest	Quantitative	Very difficult	Difficult	Easy
33	Match	Other	Very easy	Very easy	Very easy
34	Over	Spatial	Very easy	Very easy	Very easy
35	As Many	Quantitative	Easy	Very easy	Very easy
36	Third	Quantitative	Easy	Very easy	Very easy
37	Pther	Other	Very easy	Very easy	Very easy
38	Starting	Temporal	Very easy	Very easy	Very easy
39	Most	Quantitative	Very easy	Very easy	Very easy
40	Behind	Spatial	Very easy	Very easy	Very easy
41	Left	Spatial	Difficult	Difficult	Easy
42	Between	Spatial	Easy	Very easy	Very easy
43	Different	Quantitative	Very easy	Very easy	Very easy
44	Pair	Quantitative	Easy	Very easy	Very easy
45	Below	Spatial	Very easy	Very easy	Very easy
46	Skip	Spatial	Difficult	Difficult	Easy
47	Forward	Spatial	Difficult	Easy	Very easy
48	Least	Quantitative	Difficult	Easy	Very easy
49	Backward	Spatial	Easy	Very easy	Very easy
50	Equal	Quantitative	Difficult	Easy	Very easy

TABLE 3.3 **Concepts by Type and Level of Difficulty (Spanish)—Fall Testing**

Item No.	Concept	Type of Concept	Level of Difficulty Kindergarten	1st Grade	2nd Grade
1	Más alto	Spatial	Easy	Very easy	Very easy
2	El centro	Spatial	Difficult	Easy	Easy
3	Completo(a)	Quantitative	Easy	Very easy	Very easy
4	Al lado	Spatial	Difficult	Easy	Very easy
5	Ultimo	Spatial	Difficult	Very easy	Very easy
6	Mediano	Quantitative	Difficult	Difficult	Very easy
7	Siempre	Temporal	Easy	Very easy	Very easy
8	Derecha	Spatial	Very difficult	Very difficult	Very difficult
9	Esquina	Spatial	Difficult	Very easy	Very easy
10	Antes	Temporal	Very Difficult	Very difficult	Difficult
11	Final	Spatial	Difficult	Easy	Very easy
12	Más lejos	Spatial	Easy	Very easy	Very easy
13	Parte	Quantitative	Difficult	Easy	Easy
14	A través	Spatial	Very easy	Very easy	Very easy
15	Algunos(as)	Quantitative	Very difficult	Difficult	Difficult
16	Arriba	Spatial	Very easy	Very easy	Very easy
17	Separados(as)	Spatial	Difficult	Easy	Very easy
18	Primer	Quantitative	Easy	Very easy	Very easy
19	Línea	Spatial	Very easy	Very easy	Very easy
20	Pocos(as)	Quantitative	Easy	Very easy	Very easy
21	Más cerca	Spatial	Very difficult	Difficult	Easy
22	Cada	Quantitative	Difficult	Difficult	Difficult
23	Más abajo	Spatial	Very Easy	Easy	Easy
24	Nunca	Temporal	Easy	Easy	Very easy
25	Empezando	Temporal	Very difficult	Difficult	Easy
26	Segundo	Quantitative	Very difficult	Difficult	Very easy
27	En frente	Spatial	Easy	Very easy	Very easy
28	Más ancha	Quantitative	Difficult	Easy	Difficult
29	Retirado	Spatial	Difficult	Easy	Very easy
30	Mitad	Quantitative	Difficult	Difficult	Very easy
31	Iguales	Spatial	Very easy	Very easy	Very easy
32	La menor cantidad	Quantitative	Very difficult	Very difficult	Very difficult
33	Hacen juego	Other	Difficult	Difficult	Easy
34	Sobre	Spatial	Easy	Easy	Difficult
35	Tantos . . . como	Quantitative	Difficult	Easy	Very easy
36	Tercer(a)	Quantitative	Very difficult	Difficult	Easy
37	Otro	Other	Very difficult	Difficult	Difficult
38	Empezando	Temporal	Very easy	Very easy	Very easy
39	Más	Quantitative	Difficult	Easy	Very easy
40	Detrás	Spatial	Very easy	Very easy	Very easy
41	Izquierda	Spatial	Very difficult	Difficult	Very easy
42	En medio de	Spatial	Difficult	Easy	Very easy
43	Diferente	Quantitative	Easy	Very easy	Very easy
44	Par	Quantitative	Difficult	Easy	Very easy
45	Debajo	Spatial	Very easy	Very easy	Very easy
46	Sáltense	Spatial	Very difficult	Very difficult	Difficult
47	Inclinado(a)	Spatial	Very difficult	Very difficult	Easy
48	Menos	Quantitative	Difficult	Easy	Easy
49	Hacia atrás	Spatial	Very difficult	Very difficult	Easy
50	Igual	Quantitative	Difficult	Difficult	Very easy

TABLE 3.4 **Concepts by Type and Level of Difficulty (Spanish)—Spring Testing**

Item No.	Concept	Type of Concept	Level of Difficulty Kindergarten	 1st Grade	 2nd Grade
1	Más alto	Spatial	Easy	Easy	Easy
2	El centro	Spatial	Easy	Easy	Easy
3	Completa	Quantitative	Easy	Very easy	Very easy
4	Al lado	Spatial	Easy	Very easy	Very easy
5	Útimo	Spatial	Easy	Very easy	Very easy
6	Mediano	Quantitative	Difficult	Easy	Very easy
7	Siempre	Temporal	Very easy	Very easy	Very easy
8	Derecha	Spatial	Very difficult	Very difficult	Difficult
9	Esquina	Spatial	Easy	Easy	Very easy
10	Antes	Temporal	Very difficult	Difficult	Easy
11	Final	Spatial	Difficult	Very easy	Very easy
12	Más lejos	Spatial	Very easy	Very easy	Very easy
13	Parte	Quantitative	Difficult	Easy	Easy
14	A través	Spatial	Very easy	Very easy	Very easy
15	Algunos	Quantitative	Very difficult	Difficult	Difficult
16	Arriba	Spatial	Very easy	Very easy	Very easy
17	Separadas	Spatial	Easy	Easy	Very easy
18	Primer	Quantitative	Very easy	Very easy	Very easy
19	Línea	Spatial	Very easy	Very easy	Very easy
20	Pocos	Quantitative	Very easy	Very easy	Very easy
21	Más cerca	Spatial	Difficult	Difficult	Difficult
22	Cada	Quantitative	Very difficult	Difficult	Easy
23	Más abajo	Spatial	Very easy	Very easy	Very easy
24	Nunca	Temporal	Difficult	Easy	Very easy
25	Empezando	Temporal	Very difficult	Difficult	Easy
26	Segundo	Quantitative	Difficult	Easy	Easy
27	En frente	Spatial	Very easy	Very easy	Very easy
28	Más ancha	Quantitative	Difficult	Easy	Easy
29	Retirado	Spatial	Easy	Easy	Easy
30	Mitad	Quantitative	Difficult	Easy	Very easy
31	Iguales	Spatial	Very easy	Very easy	Very easy
32	La menor cantidad	Quantitative	Very difficult	Difficult	Very difficult
33	Hacen juego	Other	Difficult	Easy	Difficult
34	Sobre	Spatial	Easy	Easy	Very easy
35	Tantos . . . como	Quantitative	Easy	Very easy	Easy
36	Tercera	Quantitative	Very difficult	Easy	Very easy
37	Otro	Other	Difficult	Easy	Easy
38	Empezando	Temporal	Very easy	Very easy	Very easy
39	Más	Quantitative	Easy	Very easy	Very easy
40	Detrás	Spatial	Very easy	Very easy	Very easy
41	Izquierda	Spatial	Very difficult	Very difficult	Very difficult
42	En medio de	Spatial	Easy	Easy	Very easy
43	Diferente	Quantitative	Easy	Very easy	Very easy
44	Par	Quantitative	Difficult	Easy	Very easy
45	Debajo	Spatial	Very easy	Very easy	Very easy
46	Sáltense	Spatial	Very difficult	Very difficult	Very difficult
47	Inclinado	Spatial	Very difficult	Very difficult	Very difficult
48	Menos	Quantitative	Difficult	Easy	Easy
49	Hacia atrás	Spatial	Very difficult	Difficult	Difficult
50	Igual	Quantitative	Difficult	Easy	Very easy

organized in the *Teacher Observations of Basic Concept Use Across Curriculum Areas* section of the *Test Summary and Teacher Observation Form* by curriculum area, including concepts needed

- to follow teacher directions and participate in classroom activities,
- for mathematics and science,
- for reading (story sequences, book knowledge, and phonemic awareness) and
- in general.

Suggestions for Using the Results in Intervention

Basic concepts are often used in combination with other concepts in problem solving. As students move from using concepts at concrete levels to applying them at more abstract and thought-provoking levels, these concepts become increasingly important to comprehension, reasoning, and thinking skills in general. Basic concepts are components of tasks that involve

- classification (e.g., *tallest, highest, widest*),
- taking the perspective of another (e.g., *in front* of or *behind* a table), and
- seriation (e.g., *first, second, third*).

Students who respond correctly to concepts assessed with *Forms E* and *F,* and who are familiar with easier concepts may be challenged when they are required to process and respond to directions that involve two or more concepts used in combination. For example, the teacher may ask students to "Mark *all* of the words in the *top row* that *begin* with the letter *B,*" or to make intermediate position comparisons such as "Mark the basket with *more* apples than *one* basket, but *fewer* apples than *another* basket." Such activities help identify students who can respond to concepts correctly when presented individually, but who encounter difficulty when the same concepts are combined with other concepts. Instructions such as these involve a student's ability to

- attend to, remember, and coordinate more than one basic concept at a time;
- identify similarities; and
- make difficult comparisons.

The instructions you use can help students build upon the ways in which they are able to apply concepts, and identify the kinds of difficulties they encounter. You can expand students' depth and scope of concept usage with instructions that

- encourage the use of concepts in combination (e.g., "Point to the *last* box in the *second* row");
- focus attention on opposites (e.g., *left-right, top-bottom*);

- focus attention on degree (e.g., *far, farther, farthest*);
- express concepts through more than one sense modality (for example, a *high table* and a *high musical note*, in the visual and auditory modalities, respectively);
- use basic concepts to classify;
- use concepts to order situations and events of increasing length;
- consider special characteristics of selected concepts, such as cross-laterality with *right-left;*
- use probes to help students bring meaning from long term memory;
- use concepts to compare something to a standard; and
- consider the effect of different linguistic constructions on a student's use of concepts. For example, "Move the chair *before* you move the box" is easier for students to follow than "Move the box *after* you move the chair."

The imaginative teacher will find many ways to supplement these suggestions and to incorporate them into a teaching program especially designed to meet local needs and take into account the diversity of the students served.

Using Multiple Procedures to Assess Students' Concept Understanding

To address the issues inherent in assessing students' concept understanding raised above, Boehm (1991) proposed a multiple-step model for assessing basic concepts. This model incorporates a blend of norm-referenced and continuous monitoring approaches recommended by Ysseldyke and Thurlow (1984) including error analysis, observation, and clinical interviewing. The steps include:

1. using tests such as the Boehm–3 to survey of a large number of basic concepts;
2. reviewing the patterns of a student's errors on the test;
3. observing over time the student's spontaneous use of basic concepts and ability to generalize these concepts across contexts;
4. engaging in a brief *strategy interview* with the student to identify the strategies the he or she uses to arrive at answers; and
5. engaging in a "mini-teach" to determine how ready the student is to learn a concept and the adult support needed to be successful.

Steps 1 through 3 have been built into the procedures suggested in this manual. Steps 4 and 5 should be helpful, although time constraints may limit their use in the classroom. These steps are particularly important for other evaluators (e.g., the speech-language pathologist, school psychologist, reading specialist, and educational diagnostician) to understand how students arrive at their answers, their strengths, and where their skills/knowledge breaks down.

An additional 5 to 10 minutes at the end of the same session (if the test is individually administered, or a few days later) with the student can be useful in helping evaluators refine their hypotheses and develop intervention strategies. The *strategy interview* mentioned in step 4 is based on Piaget's (1929) clinical interview and involves posing questions to probe students' responses without suggesting answers. The evaluator selects two or three items the child has answered correctly and incorrectly and, using an unmarked response form, repeats the test question. After the student has responded by pointing, the evaluator may ask such questions as

> "How did you figure out your answer?"
>
> "How did you know you were right?"
>
> "How would you explain this to a little kid?"
>
> "Why wasn't this one right?"

The interview continues with each probe based on the student's previous response until the evaluator has a better understanding of how the student arrived at his or her answer. Although a frequent first response is "I don't know," most students respond. They often reveal related language, when concepts are stable or emerging, and useful strategies for eliminating incorrect responses.

Some of the misunderstandings uncovered by this method may be rather subtle. However, personal interviews with students who participated in the pre-standardization tryout of items yielded a number of typical errors. These are summarized below to provide the teacher with an idea of the kinds of errors that may be expected of students in kindergarten and first grade.

- Some students responded with the polar opposite of the concept tested. ("It's littlest because it's biggest," or "It's the widest because it's little and kind of skinny.")
- Some marked more than one choice so that confusion was suggested.
- Some responded to only part of the direction.
- Some had no notion of the concept and guessed.
- Some were reported by their teachers to be familiar with a similar concept term, but not the *target* concept term.

A response with the opposite concept was the most frequent error made among the students interviewed. This type of error suggests partial knowledge of the concept tested and confusion due to poor establishment of the concept or the concept label.

Students who answered correctly were generally able to do one or more of the following:

- Describe the answer by using a synonymous concept label. ("It's widest because it's biggest.")
- Eliminate choices within an item as incorrect. ("It wasn't the longest or the littlest one.")

- Specifically point out cues used in pictures. ("It's in front of the dog because his head is looking at it.")

The "mini-teach" enables the evaluator to teach concepts, step by step, using familiar concrete objects, and pointing out relevant features. Some students grasp the concept immediately, indicating that they had not been exposed to the concept term previously, but understand the concept. Other students pick up aspects of the concept and show where instruction needs to start.

Attention is increasingly being directed towards understanding the cognitive processes that underlie task performance and the strategies students use to solve problems (Kintsch, 1998; Lidz, 1983, 1991; Peverly & Kitzen 1998). This information can be useful for intervention and is relevant to the assessment of basic concepts (Boehm, 2000). What processes, for example, underlie successful performance or are the sources of difficulty? Based on your observations, the strategy interview, and mini-teach discussed earlier, consider the student's behavior and the suggestions that follow for task presentation and intervention.

Does the student. . .	If not, then . . .
orient to the task?	allow sufficient warm-up time for the student to focus attention.
understand the purpose of the task?	work with practice items until the student understands.
pay attention to the spoken direction?	draw attention to the task with game-like prompts like "**Ready**?" If culturally appropriate, gain eye contact.
respond only after you finish the direction?	hold the student's hand until the direction is presented; say "**Wait until I finish.**"
remember the direction?	repeat the direction if necessary.
attempt the task?	stress key words if needed.
want to try?	prompt student with "**Give it a try,**" "**Guess,**" or "**I bet you can do it.**" Consider what prompts, praise, or other reinforcers are needed for the student to be successful.
look at the pictures and respond?	encourage the student to look at the picture(s).
eliminate options?	engage in a mini-teach, breaking down the task as needed.
respond quickly?	give the student lots of time and prompts to respond as necessary.

Using the previous material as general background, the teacher may move naturally from discussions of error analyses into activities designed to increase the *depth* and *scope* of the student's understanding. The various meanings and connotations of a concept may be explored, as well as its use in different situations and contexts. *The Boehm Resource Guide for Basic Concept Teaching* was developed to provide activity suggestions, game cards, picture cards, and other practice materials to enhance the depth and scope of concept usage, and to encourage the use of basic concepts for reasoning and dealing with more complex problems. These activities can be modified to reflect the creativity of the teacher and the culture and interests of the students involved. Development of the *Resource Guide* was guided by the work of Piaget, Gagné, and Klausmeier. Each unit in the *Resource Guide* presents concept activities at increasing levels of complexity. This spiraling approach allows the teacher to select activities to match individual needs. Many activities are challenging for students in second grade and above. This approach to concept development is supported by Bagnato, Neisworth, and Munson (1989), Klausmeier (1992), and other research.

Sequence of Concept Presentation

The sequence of concept presentation followed in the *Resource Guide* that the teacher may find useful to build into concept activities is as follows:

- present the concept in relationship to the student's own body;
- present the concept through the use of concrete materials;
- specifically label the concept;
- use the concept in several concrete situations so that the label does not become tied to one object or situation;
- show a representation of the concept in photographs or simple pictures;
- use the concept to respond to line drawings typical of the printed page;
- encourage the student to use the concept term in everyday activities;
- encourage the student to form mental pictures relevant to the concept and describe these to others;
- use a concept in combination with other concepts; and
- apply concepts at more abstract levels to make comparisons, sequence, and solve problems.

As students gain a firmer grasp of basic concepts, the teacher can introduce concepts that are used in different ways and that fall into more than one category. For example, students can be taught that *through* has the meaning of "finished" as well as its directional meaning. They can be shown the various applications of the concept *corner*; and they can discover that an object can be both *short* and *long*, depending upon the reference object with which it is compared. (The multiple classification of items by context category in Tables 3.1–3.4, and on the *Individual Summary and Observation Form* will help you identify concepts with several meanings and the contexts in which they are used.)

Strategies to Consider in Teaching Concepts

Based on the results of past research (Clark, 1971; Klausmeier, 1976, 1992; Tennysson & Cocchiarella, 1986; Tennyson & Park, 1980), a number of strategies for successful concept teaching have been identified.

Teaching Opposites or Concept Pairs (e.g., top-bottom)

- Present and label three or four examples of one member of the concept pair (*top*).
- Present and label three or four examples of the opposite member of the concept pair (*bottom*).
- Present and label three or four mixed examples where both members of the concept pair are illustrated (both *top* and *bottom*).
- Request students to verbalize the concept label throughout the task.
- Allow students to physically manipulate objects that illustrate the concept.
- Ask students to identify the concept relationship with respect to other objects in their environment (find the *top* and *bottom* of objects, or move objects to the *top* and *bottom* of others).
- Provide immediate feedback to students about the correctness of their responses.

Additional Considerations For Concepts That Are Not Opposites (e.g., pair)

- Present three or four illustrations in which the student sees both an example and a non-example of the target concept (a *pair* of shoes and a single pencil).
- Define the critical attribute(s) that highlight the concept (a *pair* is two things of a kind).
- Practice the concept in a variety of contexts.

It is important that these activities are presented using interesting objects or situations, such as art, music, and play; not as drill.

Another important consideration for instruction is the fact that students able to point to or act out correct examples of basic concept relationships do not necessarily use these same concept terms in their everyday language. For example, Meissner (1973, 1975) found that inner city students able to respond correctly to 10 positional concepts selected from the *Boehm Test of Basic Concepts* were not able to produce these concept terms in a two-child communication task. This study showed that concept comprehension is easier than concept communication. Communication, however, improved with age. Fourth graders were better able to communicate basic concepts than second graders. A later study by Meissner (1978) found that second graders were better able to verbalize concepts than kindergartners, but verbalized correctly only three-fourths of the concepts. In contrast, French and Nelson (1985) found that very young students were able to produce temporal and causal terms in the same way as do adults when asked to tell what happens in familiar events, such as going to a restaurant or birthday party.

Pre- and Post-Intervention Testing

An especially important use of the Boehm–3 is as a post-training measure of basic concept mastery. Initial results on the Boehm–3 provide a sound basis for planning the content and sequence of training. Administration of the alternate form of the test upon completion of training then helps to indicate the progress of the students in the program or, viewed differently, the effectiveness of the intervention. *Form F* was designed to minimize the effects of practice on scores obtained on retesting. As noted earlier, training should not focus on the specific items that appear on either form of the test so that post-training test results reflect more than rote memorization.

Although *Forms E* and *F* yield comparable raw scores, the difficulty levels for most corresponding items on the two forms (those that measure the same concepts) do differ slightly. Such differences need to be taken into account when interpreting the results of studies that employ one form as a pre-training measure.

Despite these differences, the administration of alternate forms of the test as pre- and post-training measures is preferable to the repeated use of the same form, since students are thereby allowed to demonstrate their concept knowledge in more than one context. In this regard, the following points should be kept in mind:

1. Before-and-after comparisons of scores for an individual student are often difficult to interpret, and sometimes hard to justify. Consequently, the difference between pre-intervention and post-intervention scores of a particular student should be interpreted tentatively and with caution.

   Differences between a group's average performance on an item before and after training are statistically more stable than an individual's item scores, and may be used with some confidence to demonstrate group changes. These differences may reflect the overall effectiveness of a concept-training program, and provide evidence relevant to program evaluation.

2. Post-intervention scores are interpretable in themselves, without reference to pre-intervention results. For individual students, they reflect current status and may be used in the same way as pre-intervention scores. Group summaries, particularly percent passing values for individual items, may be used to identify concepts on which a class could profit from further instruction.

3. The effects of varying item difficulty values across the forms can be offset to some extent if half of the students in a given group receive *Form E* as a pre-intervention measure and *Form F* as a post-intervention measure. The rest of the students are given the two forms under similar conditions, but in the reverse sequence. Such a procedure will be facilitated if two comparable classroom groups of about equal size are available. Then pre-intervention difficulty values for each of the 50 concepts may be computed by pooling the results obtained with *Forms E* and *F* given before intervention, and post-intervention difficulty values may be similarly obtained.

Through this procedure, the value of using alternate forms is retained, since no student is tested twice with the same form of the Boehm–3. The effects of different item difficulties of the two forms cancel, because the percentages of the total number of students demonstrating mastery of a given concept are based on the administration of both forms at each testing. Within the bounds imposed by error of measurement, the pre- and post-intervention differences in the percentages of students demonstrating knowledge of a concept would reflect only the effects of intervention and maturation.

How to Involve Parents in the Intervention Process

The speech-language pathologist and the teacher, or other interventionist, play a critical role in involving parents. There is an important relationship between parent involvement in a child's early language development and the child's later school achievement (Hart & Risley, 1995). In an extensive study, Hart and Risley found wide differences in the amount of talk and the richness of adult-child exchanges among families of different backgrounds. These large differences, in turn, were reflected in vocabulary development. Basic relational concepts were likely to be among the words used.

Children also imitate the specific words they hear parents and teachers use. For example, in a study of adult input on preschool children's acquisition of spatial and temporal relational concept terms, Classon (1988) found that parents and teachers predominantly used *more-less* in a quantitative, as opposed to temporal sense and generated fewer examples of *less*. As a result, children in this study were most able to use *more* and least able to use *less*. Pianta, Nimetz, and Bennett (1997) also found that the quality, as well as the quantity, of the adult-child exchange is important for basic concept development.

The *Parent Report Form*, which can be detached from the *Record Form*, includes general suggestions for ways in which the parent can help the child learn basic concepts. It is often useful to suggest one or two specific activities that the parent can carry out through an enjoyable exchange. These activities should involve concepts that appear to be emerging in the student's receptive and/or expressive language. The child may be able to acquire these concepts more easily than other concepts not currently in the student's language repertoire and later move on to other new concepts.

Ongoing involvement with parents focusing on individual concepts of interest is useful. A page of simple age appropriate activities involving a particular concept can be sent home with the student. Regular parent workshops can be scheduled where parents can share their successful at-home activities and new ideas for working on concepts can be presented.

Chapter 4
Development and Standardization of the English Edition

Developing the Test

The first steps in the revision of Boehm–R involved reviewing the research literature in basic concept acquisition and gathering additional information from Boehm–R customers.

Concepts used in early reading and mathematics curricula, in teachers' verbal instructions, and in standardized test directions were collected and frequency counts were calculated. Concepts consistently used across a number of pre-kindergarten, kindergarten, first- and second-grade curricula were identified and compared to concepts tested in Boehm–R. Based on these activities, new concepts were added to form the Boehm–3 tryout version.

Information From User Surveys

A survey was mailed to Boehm–R customers during the winter of 1997. Seventy-six percent of the respondents were classroom teachers, special educators, early intervention teachers, speech-language pathologists, or school psychologists. Twenty-four percent of the respondents were other school personnel (i.e., test directors, school counselors, and educational diagnosticians). Survey results indicated that more than 50% of Boehm–R users administer the test as part of a diagnostic battery to qualify a student for services, to assist with determining objectives after enrollment in services, and as a post test to assess intervention or curriculum effectiveness. The primary comments from survey respondents included the need for more difficult test items; updated, clearer pictures; and more appropriate wording (decreased linguistic complexity) of certain test items. Information about the manual, user-friendliness, "problem" items, and scoring was compiled so that appropriate changes could be made to the existing Boehm–R.

Bias Reviews of Boehm–R

All the current Boehm–R items were subjected to multiple reviews by clinicians and teachers experienced in working with children with a wide range of ability levels. Experts in the field of child assessment and bias issues reviewed all items. A review panel comprised of individuals in the areas of education, speech pathology, and psychology were instructed to review items for the following types of bias.

- *Gender* (e.g., items that use the terms *man* or *mankind* to represent humanity or the use of *he* or *him* as a general referent)
- *Ethnic* (items that show bias through visual stimuli, such as a lack of minority-group representation or a lack of variety within minority groups)
- *Class* (items that express socioeconomic bias, such as a sentence about the purchase of a very expensive sports car or other luxury item)
- *Cultural* (items that portray situations or vocabulary to which children from certain cultures may not have been exposed to or experienced)
- *Regional* (items that use terms not commonly used nationwide, for example "brown paper bag" might be known as "sack," "tote," or "poke" in different parts of the country)

The expert panel of bias reviewers of Boehm–R included:

Andrea S. Canter, PhD
Lead Psychologist
Minneapolis Public School District
Minneapolis, MN

Li-Rong Lilly Cheng, PhD
Assistant Dean of the Global Development Program
San Diego State University
San Diego, CA

Peggy F. Crowell, PhD
Executive Director of Student Services
Jackson Public Schools
Jackson, MS

Charles A. Espalin, PhD
Director of Counseling Services
Los Angeles Unified School District
Los Angeles, CA

Betty Nunnery, M.S., CCC-SLP
Speech-Language Pathologist
Adams 12 School District
Thornton, CO

Salvador Hector Ochoa, PhD
Associate Professor
Department of Educational Psychology
Texas A&M University, College of Education
College Station, TX

Toya Wyatt, PhD
Associate Professor
California State University at Fullerton
Fullerton, CA

Gary Yung
Assessment Specialist
Assessment and Evaluation Department
San Francisco Unified School District
San Francisco, CA

Findings of this panel of Boehm–R reviewers included the following:

- Children consisted of either all girls or all boys, or at best, presented poor ratios of girls to boys when portrayed in groups.
- Girls were often portrayed wearing dresses.
- Boys were portrayed as leaders, and girls were not.
- Many of the toys were "male associated."
- There was very little ethnic diversity.
- Some ethnic groups were not represented.
- Some of the words used were regional or unfamiliar to children in some areas of the country (e.g., tunnel, *mark* an "X" vs. *put* an "X", *at* the corner vs. *in* the corner).

Representatives of The Psychological Corporation offices in the United Kingdom, Canada, and Australia also reviewed the items. Their comments were similar to those made by the bias review panel. Comments from all of the reviewers were compiled and recommendations for item changes related to gender, ethnicity, cultural, and regional issues were incorporated in the revision.

Tryout Item Development

After review of the concepts used in preschool and early school curricula, five new items were added. These items included *least*, *ahead*, *longest*, *backward*, and *equal*. Some items were tried out in both the Boehm–3 and the preschool editions of the test. The overlapping items, including *top*; *next*; *away*; *different*; *in front*; *most*; *before*; *farthest*; *last*; *bottom*; *some, but not many*; *first*; *between*; and *least*, function as a bridge between the two versions of the test.

The linguistic complexity of the test directions was minimized as much as possible, as with previous editions of Boehm. The concepts *in, on, up, down, off, little,* and *another* are used in the Boehm–3 directions. Based on field tests results of the original Boehm–Preschool, nearly all children know these concepts by the age of 5 years. Some of the directions given to the children at the beginning of the test include multiple concepts. For example, the teacher says to the children, "Now take your finger off the little box with the candle in it and pick up your pencil." Teachers or other assessors may model the desired behavior to minimize the complexity of the directions.

Instructions for each test item are presented twice. The first presentation enables the student to orient to the correct picture, and the second presentation enables the student to process/verify the instructions. Repetition of instructions also reduces memory load.

Selection of concepts to be tested was also based on how easily they could be depicted. For example, concepts such as *big* and *little* lend themselves well to pictorial representation, while *hard* and *soft* are more difficult to portray within the small space for each item in the test booklet. Item contexts that depicted an activity familiar to students across cultures and socioeconomic groups were developed for the tryout version of Boehm–3. All items from Boehm–R were redrawn to update the illustrations and are presented in color. Boehm–R test items that involved situations unfamiliar to young children (e.g., taking a car for repairs), or race or gender stereotypes (e.g., only boys as "leaders") were corrected or deleted.

Developing Parallel Forms for Tryout

To develop the tryout version of Boehm–3, parallel items on Boehm–R *Forms C* and *D* were reviewed. The percent of students passing each parallel item, or *p*-values, were examined. Additionally, items were reviewed to determine if each had the same number, type, and location of foils to ensure that items were as parallel as possible. If discrepancies were found, the following kinds of adjustments were made:

- Number of foils was adjusted
- Location of foils was adjusted
- Orientation of the pictures was adjusted
- Item context was changed by altering the pictures

If there was a large difference between the percent of students passing the same item on Boehm–R *Form C* versus *Form D*, or if an item was significantly changed based on customer or reviewer suggestions, a third item context was developed to test the concept. A third context (parallel) item was developed for 40 of the 50 Boehm–R items. The two items closest in difficulty would be chosen for the standardization. Items were constructed that incorporated familiar vocabulary and depicted familiar situations for students.

The Boehm–3 tryout forms were labeled as *Form E, Booklets 1 and 2* and *Form F, Booklets 1 and 2*. Each form included 88 test items. Fifty items were revisions of Boehm–R items, 30 were additional items measuring the same concept, and 8 items were either new or modifications of the more difficult items from the preschool version of Boehm *(Boehm-Preschool)*. Ten of the 30 alternate items were included on both *Forms E* and *F* to serve as linking items so that students' performance on *Forms E* and *F* could be compared during data analysis.

Teachers were instructed to give students a break between administration of the booklets. Booklet 1 included the revisions of Boehm–R items; Booklet 2 included the new alternate items, concepts new to the test, and difficult concepts from *Boehm-Preschool*.

Tryout Testing

Item tryout testing began in October 1998. The Boehm–3 tryout version was administered to a group of students representative of the demographics of the United States. A bias over-sample also was collected. An over-sample involves collecting a large number of "extra" cases (in addition to those needed to approximate the demographic requirements), so that there is a sufficient number of minority students to complete a statistical analysis of bias. Bias studies were conducted to see if different groups of students performed differently on the test.

The purpose of the tryout was to

- identify items that students found difficult for reasons other than lack of concept knowledge, such as ambiguous wording or unclear artwork;
- identify items that were answered correctly by most students in kindergarten, first, and second grades;
- identify items that might be unfair or offensive to particular groups of young students;
- observe item progression by grade; and
- find item representations or wording that presented special difficulty in the Spanish version.

More than 5,000 kindergarten, first-, and second-grade students participated in the nationwide tryout of Boehm–3. Teachers who were examiners for this study were instructed to test all the students in their classrooms. Therefore, students who received special services, but were mainstreamed in regular classrooms, were included in the tryout. An attempt was made to test students representative of a variety of school district sizes and socioeconomic levels. Students from urban, suburban, and rural areas, as well as non-public schools, also were tested. Approximately half of the students were administered *Form E* and the remainder were administered *Form F*. Appendix B lists the districts and non-public schools from which the tryout data were collected.

Tables 4.1 through 4.5 show the demographic characteristics of the tryout sample. Some tables include *NR*. This indicates that for whatever reason, this information was not reported at the time of testing. Table 4.1 shows the distribution of the tryout sample by grade and form.

TABLE 4.1 Boehm–3 Tryout Sample by Grade and Form

	Form E		*Form F*		**Total**
Grade	*n*	%	*n*	%	*n*
K	727	27.4	737	29.6	1,464
1	1,037	39.1	880	35.3	1,917
2	859	32.3	869	34.9	1,728
NR	33	1.2	6	.2	39
Total	2,656	100.0	2,492	100.0	5,148

Table 4.2 shows the distribution of the tryout sample by gender and form. For the purpose of this study, the number of students of each gender is considered to be equally divided.

TABLE 4.2 **Boehm–3 Tryout Sample by Gender and Form**

	Form E		*Form F*	
Gender	*n*	%	*n*	%
Female	1,261	47.5	1,201	48.2
Male	1,373	51.7	1,282	51.4
NR	22	.8	9	.4
Total	2,656	100.0	2,492	100.0

Table 4.3 shows the racial/ethnic distribution of the students in the tryout sample by form. For the purposes of this study, the category of "other" includes students of Asian, Native American, and Pacific Islander descent and all other students not part of the other groups.

TABLE 4.3 **Boehm–3 Tryout Sample by Race/Ethnicity and Form**

	Form E		*Form F*		**U.S. Population**
Race/Ethnicity	*n*	%	*n*	%	%
African-American	499	18.8	537	21.5	16.5
Hispanic	314	11.8	229	9.2	16.3
Other	57	2.1	105	4.2	5.0
White	1,648	62.1	1,568	62.9	62.2
NR	138	5.2	53	2.2	—
Total	2,656	100.0	2,492	100.0	100.0

U.S. Bureau of the Census. (1998). *Current population survey, October 1998: School Enrollment Supplement File* [Machine-readable data file]. Washington, DC: U.S. Bureau of the Census (Producer/Distributor).

Table 4.4 shows the geographical distribution of the tryout sample by form.

TABLE 4.4 **Boehm–3 Tryout Sample by Region and Form**

	Form E		*Form F*		**U.S. Population**
Region	*n*	%	*n*	%	%
Northeast	521	19.6	500	20.0	19.0
North Central	529	19.9	484	19.4	22.5
South	957	36.0	881	35.4	34.5
West	649	24.5	627	25.2	24.0
Total	2,656	100.0	2,492	100.0	100.0

U.S. Bureau of the Census. (1998). *Current population survey, October 1998: School Enrollment Supplement File* [Machine-readable data file]. Washington, DC: U.S. Bureau of the Census (Producer/Distributor).

A variety of school districts representing three socioeconomic levels were invited to participate in the tryout version of Boehm–3. The levels were determined by reviewing the income level and education of residents within a defined school district. These classifications (low, middle, and high) were designed to place 33% of the public school district population into each of the 3 categories. This index was based on the *1992–93 National Center for Educational Statistics Public Agency data tape*. Students participating in tryout testing who attend non-public schools were included as the separate category. Table 4.5 reports the distribution of school districts included in the study, according to socioeconomic level of the school district and form.

TABLE 4.5 **Boehm–3 Tryout Sample by Socioeconomic Level of the School District and Non-public Schools and Form**

Socioeconomic Level	Form E *n*	Form E %	Form F *n*	Form F %
Low	1,022	38.5	982	39.4
Middle	586	22.1	639	25.6
High	807	30.4	657	26.4
Non-public schools	241	9.0	214	8.6
Total	2,656	100.0	2,492	100.0

Tryout Teacher Survey Results

Teachers who participated in the tryout testing completed surveys that included questions about the appropriateness of item wording, how well the illustrations depicted the test question, and familiarity of context used to test the target concept. The survey also posed questions about the practice items. Specifically, teachers were asked about

- the clarity of the administration directions,
- the best items and illustrations,
- whether the illustrations showed, not just diversity, but also a variety of heights, weights, and differently-abled students.

Teachers were also asked

- if the vocabulary was at age level,
- if the concepts reflected curricula,
- if all the essential concepts were included,
- if the illustrations were engaging and appropriate for students, and
- if the test results would be useful for instructional planning.

Teachers were asked to identify what they liked and disliked about the test and problem items. Additional comments about test administration times were collected. Both multiple choice and open-ended questions were included on the questionnaire. In general, teachers liked the test items and the illustrations. They commented that the situations pictured were familiar and interesting to their students. Kindergarten teachers were concerned about the difficulty of some of the concepts tested, noting that not all of the concepts had been addressed in the kindergarten curriculum. Second-grade teachers generally thought that the content was easy for their students.

As discussed earlier, the test was also submitted to multiple outside experts to evaluate possible bias or stereotyping by gender, culture, or ethnicity, and to comment on items that might be otherwise objectionable.

Specific comments and revision suggestions were compiled for each test item. Some comments related to the illustrations (e.g., "Several students thought the red flowers were strawberries"); other comments related to the difficulty of the item or the wording of the administration directions. Each item was reviewed with the results of information from the survey and the expert bias panel in mind. Items that presented problems were either modified or not included in the standardization version.

Selecting Test Items for Standardization

Both qualitative information (teacher and bias reviewer comments) and quantitative information (tryout data, statistical analysis of bias) were used in selecting items for the standardization version.

Review of *p*-values and Item Difficulty

The selection process for test items for standardization included a number of steps. Each form tested the same concepts, but in different contexts in each form. Ten items that consisted of the same target and the same context appeared on both *Forms E* and *F*. Because a large, representative sample of students took either *Form E* or *Form F*, these common items were used to put the item *p*-values (percent of students passing an item) on a common metric. This ensures that items are viewed on the same scale.

The resulting adjusted *p*-values and item difficulties were used to compare the three parallel test items across both forms. In addition to *p*-values, item-total correlations were examined. Items with poor item-total correlations were deleted. After comparing *p*-values across the three parallel items, the two items that were the closest in difficulty were selected for standardization.

Examining Bias in Tryout Items

A second group of bias reviewers examined test materials while the items were being tested. Bias reviewers were selected because of their expertise in assessment issues for non-mainstream populations. The reviewers provided written, detailed critiques of the test items and art. They reviewed all aspects of the test looking for indications of gender, ethnicity, socioeconomic, cultural, and regional bias as described earlier in this chapter.

The expert panel of reviewers of the Boehm–3 tryout version included:

Edgarita Long, PhD, CCC-SLP
Assistant Professor
Communication Disorders Program
University of Arkansas
Fayetteville, AR

Ravi Nigam, PhD, CCC-SLP
Assistant Professor of Communication Disorders
Texas Tech University Health Science Center
Lubbock, TX

Luis Riquelme, M.S., CCC-SLP
Assistant Professor
Department of Communication Sciences and Disorders
Long Island University—Brooklyn Campus
Brooklyn, NY

Christine Vining
Associate Director
Project Na'nitin
Albuquerque, NM

Toya Wyatt, PhD
Associate Professor
California State University at Fullerton
Fullerton, CA

Zheng Zhou, PhD
Assistant Professor
Department of Psychology St. John's University
Jamaica, NY

The reviewers provided the following feedback:

- Some contexts lacked familiarity for students of a particular grade.
- Possible cultural bias was noted (e.g., "spaghetti" may be less familiar to Asian children than "noodles").
- Body types of the children depicted in the illustrations were average and not varied (i.e., no depiction of very thin or heavy children).
- Some vocabulary was unfamiliar (e.g., petals of a flower).
- Some regional vocabulary was noted (e.g., "bucket" vs. "pail," "faucet" vs. "spigot").

After tryout testing was completed, items were reviewed for bias again. All of the comments from the bias review panel were considered. If an item was identified as biased, it was not used for standardization. There was one exception. If bias reviewers recommended specific changes to the illustrations or administration directions that alleviated the bias, the item was adjusted and then included in standardization.

Examining Bias Through Statistical Analyses of Tryout Data

When people think about unfair test items, they generally think about race or ethnic bias in which a specific race or minority group is depicted in a way that is stereotypic or inappropriate. However, that is only one aspect of test bias. An item may be considered unfair if students with similar skills performed differently on an item due to their group membership. The bias reviewers' comments and recommendations were compiled and reviewed in conjunction with the tryout data. In addition to reviewer comments, the empirical data were analyzed using the Mantel-Haenszel procedure, which is a statistical means of evaluating bias.

Finalizing Item Order for Standardization

Once items were selected for standardization, teacher feedback was reviewed and minor modifications were made to the wording of the verbal prompt or to the illustrations. Test items were reordered, with the easiest items placed on the first page, then easy and difficult items interspersed through the remainder of the test. Test pages were checked to ensure that there was only one example of a target illustration on a page. For example, if the test item read "Look at the ducks," there would only be one item with ducks on the page.

Standardization Testing

National fall norms were developed for the Boehm–3 by administering *Forms E* and *F* to students in kindergarten, first-, and second-grade in October and November of 1999. National spring testing to establish norms took place in April and May of 2000. Students were tested in their regular classrooms at public and private schools. A variety of school districts were invited to participate in the standardization testing. An attempt was made to test students from schools representative of the nation as a whole in terms of school district size (from 600 to more than 20,000 students), socioeconomic level of the residents of the school district, urbanicity (urban, suburban, rural, or non-public), and geographic region. Teachers who were examiners for this study were instructed to test their entire classroom of students. Therefore, students who received special services, but were mainstreamed in regular classrooms were included in the standardization.

Description of the Fall and Spring Samples

More than 11,000 students in the United States participated in the fall standardization and the related reliability and validity studies for the English and Spanish editions of the Boehm–3 and more than 7,000 students participated in the spring standardization and validity studies. Some students were dropped from the standardization study in order to meet the U.S. population demographics. (Development and standardization of the Boehm–3 Spanish edition is discussed in Chapter 5.) The Boehm–3 fall standardization sample consisted of over 6,000 students in kindergarten, first, and second-grade classrooms and the spring sample included more than 4,000 students. Tables 4.6 through 4.11 report the demographic characteristics of the English sample.

Table 4.6 reports the number of students by grade and form for the fall standardization sample. Table 4.7 depicts the spring standardization sample.

TABLE 4.6 **Boehm–3 Standardization Sample by Grade and Form—Fall Testing**

	Form E		*Form F*	
Grade	*n*	%	*n*	%
Kindergarten	960	34.0	1,055	33.0
First Grade	982	34.0	1,105	35.0
Second Grade	924	32.0	1,029	32.0
Total	2,866	100.0	3,189	100.0

TABLE 4.7 **Boehm–3 Standardization Sample by Grade and Form—Spring Testing**

	Form E		*Form F*	
Grade	*n*	%	*n*	%
Kindergarten	813	34.6	748	34.1
First Grade	829	35.3	731	33.3
Second Grade	706	30.1	717	32.6
Total	2,348	100.0	2,196	100.0

Table 4.8 shows the distribution of the fall standardization sample by gender and form. Table 4.9 depicts the spring standardization sample.

TABLE 4.8 **Boehm–3 Standardization Sample by Gender and Form—Fall Testing**

	Form E		*Form F*	
Gender	*n*	%	*n*	%
Female	1,180	41.2	1,623	50.9
Male	1,653	57.7	1,522	47.7
Not Reported	33	1.1	44	1.4
Total	2,866	100.0	3,189	100.0

TABLE 4.9 **Boehm–3 Standardization Sample by Gender and Form—Spring Testing**

	Form E		*Form F*	
Gender	*n*	%	*n*	%
Female	1,174	50.0	1,098	50.0
Male	1,174	50.0	1,098	50.0
Total	2,348	100.0	2,196	100.0

Table 4.10 reports the fall standardization sample by race/ethnicity. For the purpose of this study, the category of "other" includes students of Asian, Native American, and Pacific Islander descent and all other students not part of the other groups. Table 4.11 depicts the spring standardization sample.

TABLE 4.10 **Boehm–3 Standardization Sample by Race/Ethnicity and Form— Fall Testing**

	Form E		*Form F*		U.S. Population
Race/Ethnicity	*n*	%	*n*	%	%
African American	462	16.1	491	15.4	16.52
Hispanic	468	16.3	475	14.9	16.32
Other	137	4.8	176	5.5	5.03
White	1,773	61.9	1,985	62.2	62.13
Not Reported	26	0.9	62	2.0	—
Total	2,866	100.0	3,189	100.0	100.00

U.S. Bureau of the Census. (1998). *Current population survey, October 1998: School Enrollment Supplement File* [Machine-readable data file]. Washington, DC: U.S. Bureau of the Census (Producer/Distributor).

TABLE 4.11 **Boehm–3 Standardization Sample by Race/Ethnicity and Form—Spring Testing**

	Form E		*Form F*		U.S. Population
Race/Ethnicity	*n*	%	*n*	%	%
African American	400	17.0	395	18.0	16.52
Hispanic	382	16.3	314	14.3	16.32
Other	129	5.5	121	5.5	5.03
White	1,437	61.2	1,366	62.2	62.13
Total	2,348	100.0	2,196	100.0	100.00

U.S. Bureau of the Census. (1998). *Current population survey, October 1998: School Enrollment Supplement File* [Machine-readable data file]. Washington, DC: U.S. Bureau of the Census (Producer/Distributor).

Schools were selected from all regions of the country to provide a representative sample based on the U. S. Bureau of the Census demographics report. The map in Figure 4.1 depicts the percentages of students in kindergarten, first, and second-grades in the four regions of the country.

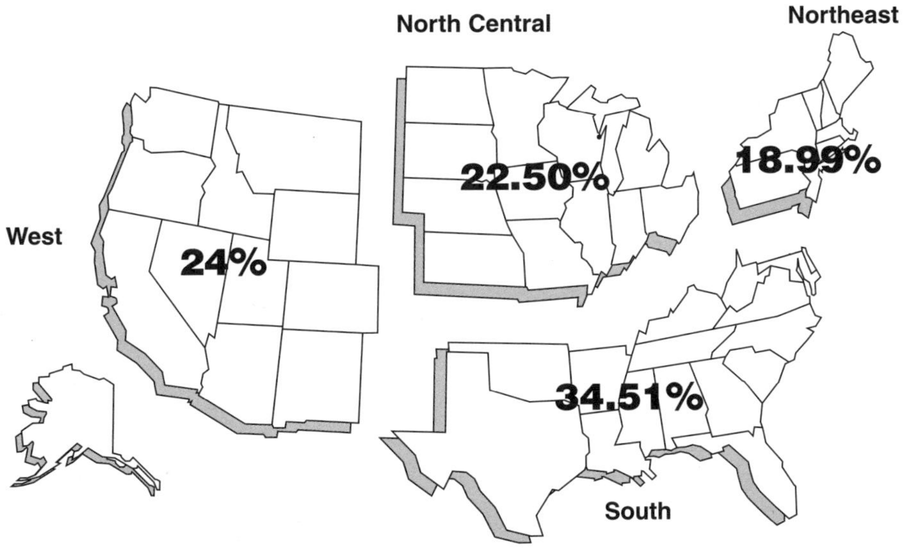

Figure 4.1 Geographic Regions of the United States for the Boehm–3 Standardization Study

U.S. Bureau of the Census. (1998). *Current population survey, October 1998: School Enrollment Supplement File* [Machine-readable data file]. Washington, DC: U.S. Bureau of the Census (Producer/Distributor).

Table 4.12 shows the geographical distribution of students participating in the fall Boehm–3 standardization study. Table 4.13 depicts the spring standardization sample. The U.S. Bureau of the Census report defines the regions.

TABLE 4.12 **Boehm–3 Standardization Sample by Region and Form—Fall Testing**

	Form E		*Form F*		U.S. Population
Region	*n*	%	*n*	%	%
Northeast	313	11.0	558	17.5	18.99
North Central	748	26.1	746	23.4	22.50
South	988	34.4	1,025	31.9	34.51
West	817	28.5	867	27.2	24.00
Total	2,866	100.0	3,189	100.0	100.00

U.S. Bureau of the Census. (1998). *Current population survey, October 1998: School Enrollment Supplement File* [Machine-readable data file]. Washington, DC: U.S. Bureau of the Census (Producer/Distributor).

TABLE 4.13 **Boehm–3 Standardization Sample by Region and Form—Spring Testing**

Region	Form E *n*	Form E %	Form F *n*	Form F %	U.S. Population %
Northeast	445	19.0	415	18.9	18.99
North Central	504	21.5	496	22.6	22.50
South	802	34.1	757	34.5	34.51
West	597	25.4	528	24.0	24.00
Total	2,348	100.0	2,196	100.0	100.00

U.S. Bureau of the Census. (1998). *Current population survey, October 1998: School Enrollment Supplement File* [Machine-readable data file]. Washington, DC: U.S. Bureau of the Census (Producer/Distributor).

The schools participating in the standardization study were categorized by the socioeconomic level of the school district. There were three levels: low, middle, and high. The levels were determined by reviewing the income level and education of residents within a defined school district. These classifications were designed to place 33% of the public school district population into each of the three categories. This index was provided using the *1992–93 National Center for Educational Statistics Public Agency data tape*. Students participating in the standardization study who attend non-public schools were included as the fourth category. Table 4.14 reports the distribution of school districts and non-public schools included in the fall standardization study by form. Table 4.15 depicts the spring standardization study.

TABLE 4.14 **Boehm–3 Standardization Sample by Socioeconomic Level of the Participating School Districts and Non-public Schools and Form—Fall Testing**

Socioeconomic Level	Form E *n*	Form E %	Form F *n*	Form F %
Low	1,348	47.0	1,365	42.8
Middle	501	17.5	694	21.8
High	533	18.6	702	22.0
Non-public	484	16.9	428	13.4
Total	2,866	100.0	3,189	100.0

TABLE 4.15 **Boehm–3 Standardization Sample by Socioeconomic Level of the Participating School Districts and Non-public Schools and Form—Spring Testing**

Socioeconomic Level	Form E *n*	Form E %	Form F *n*	Form F %
Low	408	17.4	366	16.7
Middle	738	31.4	631	28.7
High	880	37.5	832	37.9
Non-public	322	13.7	367	16.7
Total	2,348	100.0	2,196	100.0

Table 4.16 demonstrates the urbanicity of the school districts and non-public schools that were included in the fall standardization study. Table 4.17 depicts the spring standardization study. Urbanicity can be defined as the school district's service area relative to the Metropolitan Service Area and is based on zip code of the district. There are three primary levels of urbanicity: urban, suburban, and rural. This information was obtained from the *1990–91 National Center for Educational Statistics Public Agency data tape.* The percentage of students participating from non-public schools is also included.

TABLE 4.16 **Boehm–3 Standardization Sample by Urbanicity and Form— Fall Testing**

Urbanicity	*Form E* *n*	%	*Form F* *n*	%
Urban	700	24.5	798	25.1
Suburban	775	27.0	1,056	33.1
Rural	907	31.6	907	28.4
Non-public	484	16.9	428	13.4
Total	2,866	100.0	3,189	100.0

TABLE 4.17 **Boehm–3 Standardization Sample by Urbanicity and Form—Spring Testing**

Urbanicity	*Form E* *n*	%	*Form F* *n*	%
Urban	61	2.6	86	3.9
Suburban	1407	59.9	1,219	55.5
Rural	558	23.8	524	23.9
Non-public	322	13.7	367	16.7
Total	2348	100.0	2,196	100.0

Developing Norms

Norms were developed by reviewing the *p*-values (percent of students passing), item difficulty (based on Rasch analysis), and bias of the standardization data.

Review of Standardization Data: *p*-values, Item Difficulty, and Bias Studies

The data collected from the standardization were examined by reviewing the *p*-values, item difficulty, and bias studies. A large, representative sample of students took either *Form E* or *Form F* with concepts common to both forms. The item *p*-values were used to look at item progression and compare the parallel test items across both forms. The percent of students responding correctly was analyzed by grade and across grades. In addition to *p*-values, item difficulties, based on Rasch analysis, were examined. The empirical data were analyzed using the Mantel-Haenszel procedure, which is a statistical means of evaluating bias. Items were reviewed again, taking the information regarding bias into account.

Based on an examination of all the data, five items from standardization, including *narrowest*, *several*, *after*, one form of *forward*, and *longest*, were deleted for the following reasons: to keep the test at 50 items, to choose items that were closest in *p*-values, and to eliminate one item that performed poorly in the standardization study. The final edition consists of two forms (*E* and *F*), each with 50 identical concepts, in the same order, tested in different contexts.

Table 4.12 shows the percent of students passing each item in *Form E*. Table 4.13 shows the percent of students passing each item in *Form F*.

TABLE 4.18 Percent of Students Passing Each Item by Grade, *Form E* (N = 2,866 Students Tested in the Fall Standardization and N = 2,348 Students Tested in the Spring Standardization)

		Fall			Spring		
Item	**Concept**	**K**	**1**	**2**	**K**	**1**	**2**
1	Top	97	99	99	98	100	100
2	Center	78	90	94	84	93	97
3	Whole	95	99	99	97	99	100
4	Side	87	95	98	94	98	99
5	Last	85	99	99	94	99	100
6	Medium-sized	64	80	92	78	98	94
7	Always	97	99	99	98	99	100
8	Right	58	77	86	65	78	87
9	Corner	89	98	98	92	98	98
10	Before	61	84	94	77	90	96
11	End	88	98	99	95	99	100
12	Farthest	92	97	99	94	99	99
13	Part	86	96	98	93	96	99
14	Through	98	99	99	99	99	100
15	Some	62	70	84	70	81	89
16	Above	85	94	99	91	96	99
17	Separated	63	87	96	75	94	99
18	First	93	99	99	97	100	100
19	Row	91	96	99	94	98	100
20	Few	95	99	99	97	99	100
21	Next	76	91	98	81	88	93
22	Every	72	79	89	88	96	99
23	Bottom	87	98	99	95	97	99
24	Never	69	92	98	84	95	98
25	Beginning	73	85	94	81	91	97
26	Second	61	93	97	82	96	99
27	Front	94	99	99	95	98	100
28	Widest	76	88	94	85	92	94
29	Away	93	98	99	97	99	100
30	Half	81	91	98	86	95	98
31	Alike	86	96	99	90	97	99
32	Fewest	39	63	74	48	59	80
33	Match	92	97	99	93	97	99
34	Over	93	97	98	94	97	98
35	As Many	83	93	97	91	96	98
36	Third	60	93	98	85	97	99
37	Other	71	87	93	83	90	95
38	Starting	94	97	99	95	98	99
39	Most	87	94	99	92	98	99
40	Behind	89	97	99	91	97	99
41	Left	52	71	84	62	75	87
42	Between	76	86	93	80	91	97
43	Different	95	99	99	97	99	99
44	Pair	75	90	98	86	94	97
45	Below	84	94	97	90	97	99
46	Skip	37	71	87	56	82	89
47	Forward	63	81	90	73	85	93
48	Least	58	82	92	70	86	95
49	Backward	69	84	94	80	90	96
50	Equal	42	75	92	60	87	96
n		960	982	924	813	829	706

TABLE 4.19 **Percent of Students Passing Each Item by Grade, *Form F* (*N* = 3,189 Students Tested in the Fall Standardization and *N* = 2,196 Students Tested in the Spring Standardization)**

		Fall			Spring		
Item	**Concept**	**K**	**1**	**2**	**K**	**1**	**2**
1	Top	96	99	99	98	98	99
2	Center	83	87	94	86	92	97
3	Whole	91	97	99	96	98	99
4	Side	91	97	99	95	97	99
5	Last	85	98	99	96	99	100
6	Medium-Sized	68	85	93	83	90	96
7	Always	98	99	99	99	99	99
8	Right	60	74	85	71	76	88
9	Corner	83	93	98	91	95	98
10	Before	70	86	93	82	89	96
11	End	88	96	99	94	98	99
12	Farthest	87	95	98	94	97	99
13	Part	88	97	98	94	97	99
14	Through	98	99	99	99	99	99
15	Some	76	81	91	80	85	92
16	Above	85	93	98	93	95	98
17	Separated	61	78	92	75	85	95
18	First	93	99	99	98	99	99
19	Row	89	98	99	95	98	100
20	Few	93	98	99	97	99	99
21	Next	84	95	98	83	87	94
22	Every	78	81	92	91	96	98
23	Bottom	86	96	98	92	97	99
24	Never	73	91	98	88	96	99
25	Beginning	89	95	98	93	95	98
26	Second	62	93	98	87	96	99
27	Front	96	99	99	98	99	99
28	Widest	82	92	95	89	95	97
29	Away	94	96	98	96	96	98
30	Half	76	87	97	86	91	97
31	Alike	83	93	97	90	95	98
32	Fewest	36	62	74	45	62	82
33	Match	91	97	99	95	98	99
34	Over	92	94	98	93	95	98
35	As Many	83	93	97	89	95	98
36	Third	46	87	96	76	95	96
37	Other	80	92	97	91	95	98
38	Starting	89	94	96	94	94	96
39	Most	82	93	95	90	92	96
40	Behind	89	97	99	93	98	99
41	Left	51	66	82	62	74	87
42	Between	78	88	99	84	92	96
43	Different	94	99	96	97	99	99
44	Pair	77	88	99	88	91	96
45	Below	93	96	83	95	97	99
46	Skip	39	70	90	54	74	85
47	Forward	66	78	90	72	81	92
48	Least	61	79	89	67	82	90
49	Backward	71	85	96	82	91	96
50	Equal	51	75	90	64	85	93
n		1,055	1,105	1,029	748	731	717

You may note that the corresponding percent passing values for *Forms E* and *F* indicate that most items on the two forms are nearly parallel in difficulty. In some cases however, the item testing the same concept on one form may yield somewhat different values than the corresponding item on the other form. Use caution in comparing the performances of a single group that took different forms on separate occasions. Some additional issues involved in comparing results of testing with both forms are explored in the interpretation portion of Chapter 3 of this manual.

If desired, you may compare the performance of students in your classroom passing each concept to the performance of the standardization group for each item. Use the *Class Record Form* and determine the percent of students passing in your classroom to the percent passing each concept for the appropriate form using the results of standardization testing in Tables 4.18 and 4.19 on pages 93–94 of this manual.

Raw Scores

A raw score is the total number of items the student answered correctly. Table 4.20 reports mean raw scores and standard deviations for standardization by grade and form. Mean raw scores increase across the three grades (K, 1, and 2) demonstrating the increase in understanding of basic concepts over time. The standard deviations decrease over time demonstrating that there is less variability of scores as students acquire understanding of basic concepts.

TABLE 4.20 **Mean Raw Scores and Standard Deviations by Grade and Form (*N* = 2,866 for *Form E* and *N* = 3,189 for *Form F*, Fall Testing and *N* = 2,348 for *Form E* and *N* = 2,196 for *Form F*, Spring Testing)**

	Fall		Spring	
Grade	***Form E***	***Form F***	***Form E***	***Form F***
Kindergarten				
n	960	1,055	813	748
mean	38.92	39.55	42.69	43.40
SD	7.68	7.71	6.82	6.11
First Grade				
n	982	1,105	829	731
mean	45.15	44.99	46.64	46.18
SD	4.90	5.24	3.92	5.17
Second Grade				
n	924	1,029	706	717
mean	47.80	47.73	48.44	48.23
SD	3.09	3.10	2.68	3.85

Percent Correct

The percent correct is the score that indicates the percentage of items that the student answered correctly. For example, if the student received a raw score (total number of items correct) of 48 the percent correct would be 96. Table 4.21 contains the raw score and corresponding percent correct irrespective of form, grade, language of administration, or time of testing. Alternatively, this calculation can be completed easily by doubling the raw score (because a total of 50 items were presented) to determine the percent correct.

TABLE 4.21 **Percent Correct for All Grades, Fall & Spring *Forms E* and *F***

Raw Score	% Correct	Raw Score	% Correct
50	100	25	50
49	98	24	48
48	96	23	46
47	94	22	44
46	92	21	42
45	90	20	40
44	88	19	38
43	86	18	36
42	84	17	34
41	82	16	32
40	80	15	30
39	78	14	28
38	76	13	26
37	74	12	24
36	72	11	22
35	70	10	20
34	68	9	18
33	66	8	16
32	64	7	14
31	62	6	12
30	60	5	10
29	58	4	8
28	56	3	6
27	54	2	4
26	52	1	2

Performance Range

Because no precision would be gained by examining the standardization data in smaller units, it was determined that student performance could be best described using three ranges; the upper third, middle third, and lower third. Use of a performance range makes it easier for parents to understand their child's performance in relation to his or her grade level peers. To locate the appropriate performance range, find the student's grade, then locate the Form of the test that was administered. Using the student's raw score, locate the appropriate performance range. A performance range of *1* means that the student knows the basic concepts needed to perform at grade level. A performance range of *2* means the student knows most of the basic concepts, but lacks understanding of some key concepts. A performance range of *3* means that the student's knowledge of basic concepts is extremely low and teacher and parent help is needed for the childs success in school. Table 4.22 provides the performance ranges by form and grade for fall testing, and Table 4.23 provides the same information for spring testing.

TABLE 4.22 Performance Ranges by Grade and Form—Fall Testing

Kindergarten Performance Range	*Form E* Raw Scores	*Form F* Raw Scores
1	44–50	45–50
2	38–43	39–44
3	1–37	1–38
First Grade Performance Range	***Form E* Raw Scores**	***Form F* Raw Scores**
1	49–50	49–50
2	45–48	46–48
3	1–44	1–45
Second Grade Performance Range	***Form E* Raw Scores**	***Form F* Raw Scores**
1	50	50
2	49	49
3	1–48	1–48

TABLE 4.23 Performance Ranges by Grade and Form—Spring Testing

Kindergarten Performance Range	*Form E* Raw Scores	*Form F* Raw Scores
1	47–50	47–50
2	42–46	43–46
3	1–41	1–42
First Grade Performance Range	***Form E* Raw Scores**	***Form F* Raw Scores**
1	49–50	49–50
2	47–48	46–48
3	1–46	1–45
Second Grade Performance Range	***Form E* Raw Scores**	***Form F* Raw Scores**
1	50	50
2	49	49
3	1–48	1–48

Percentile Score

Percentile norms corresponding to Boehm–3 raw scores are presented in Tables 4.24 and 4.25. Table 4.25 shows the raw scores and percentiles for students tested in the fall and spring taking *Form E*. Table 4.26 shows the raw scores and percentiles for students tested in the fall and spring taking *Form F*.

TABLE 4.24 **Percentile by Grade for *Form E* (*N* = 2,866, Fall Testing and *N* = 2,348, Spring Testing)**

	Fall Percentile			Spring Percentile		
Raw Score	**K**	**1**	**2**	**K**	**1**	**2**
50	99	99	99	99	99	99
49	98	88	69	94	82	59
48	96	75	46	87	63	35
47	92	60	27	76	46	21
46	87	48	19	67	33	13
45	80	39	13	56	23	7
44	72	32	9	48	17	4
43	65	25	7	40	13	2
42	58	21	5	35	9	1
41	53	17	3	29	8	<1
40	47	14	3	25	7	<1
39	43	11	2	22	6	<1
38	38	9	1	20	4	<1
37	34	7	1	17	3	<1
36	31	5	1	14	3	<1
35	28	4	<1	12	3	<1
34	24	3	<1	10	2	<1
33	22	2	<1	8	2	<1
32	19	2	<1	8	2	<1
31	17	2	<1	7	1	<1
30	14	1	<1	5	<1	<1
29	12	1	<1	4	<1	<1
28	11	1	<1	4	<1	<1
27	9	<1	<1	4	<1	<1
26	8	<1	<1	3	<1	<1
25	7	<1	<1	3	<1	<1
24	6	<1	<1	2	<1	<1
23	4	<1	<1	2	<1	<1
22	3	<1	<1	2	<1	<1
21	3	<1	<1	2	<1	<1
20	2	<1	<1	2	<1	<1
19	1	<1	<1	2	<1	<1
18	1	<1	<1	2	<1	<1
17	1	<1	<1	2	<1	<1
16	1	<1	<1	1	<1	<1
15 or less	<1	<1	<1	<1	<1	<1

TABLE 4.25 **Percentile by Grade for *Form F* (*N* = 3,189, Fall Testing and *N* = 2,196, Spring Testing)**

	Fall Percentile			Spring Percentile		
Raw Score	**K**	**1**	**2**	**K**	**1**	**2**
50	>99	99	99	99	99	99
49	99	91	72	95	86	60
48	96	77	47	87	67	37
47	90	62	29	77	49	20
46	82	49	20	64	37	12
45	75	38	13	54	27	8
44	68	31	9	45	20	5
43	62	24	6	37	14	3
42	56	19	4	29	11	2
41	50	15	3	25	8	2
40	44	12	2	20	6	2
39	38	10	2	16	5	2
38	34	9	2	14	4	1
37	31	8	1	13	4	<1
36	27	7	1	11	4	<1
35	24	6	1	9	4	<1
34	21	5	1	8	3	<1
33	19	4	<1	6	3	<1
32	16	4	<1	6	3	<1
31	14	3	<1	5	2	<1
30	12	2	<1	4	2	<1
29	10	2	<1	4	2	<1
28	9	1	<1	3	2	<1
27	7	1	<1	3	2	<1
26	7	1	<1	2	1	<1
25	6	1	<1	2	<1	<1
24	5	<1	<1	2	<1	<1
23	4	<1	<1	2	<1	<1
22	4	<1	<1	2	<1	<1
21	3	<1	<1	2	<1	<1
20	3	<1	<1	1	<1	<1
19	3	<1	<1	<1	<1	<1
18	2	<1	<1	<1	<1	<1
17	2	<1	<1	<1	<1	<1
16	1	<1	<1	<1	<1	<1
15	1	<1	<1	<1	<1	<1
14	1	<1	<1	<1	<1	<1
13	1	<1	<1	<1	<1	<1
12	1	<1	<1	<1	<1	<1
11	1	<1	<1	<1	<1	<1
10	1	<1	<1	<1	<1	<1
9	1	<1	<1	<1	<1	<1
8	1	<1	<1	<1	<1	<1
7	1	<1	<1	<1	<1	<1
6 or less	<1	<1	<1	<1	<1	<1

The percentile score is obtained by locating the student's raw score in the left column and finding the corresponding percentile score in the appropriate grade column, from either the fall or spring section of the table. When reviewing a student's percentile score, the percentile should be interpreted as "the student performed as well as or better than ___% of his or her grade-level peers when compared to the students in the standardization sample who took the same form of Boehm–3." It is important to note that by the end of first grade, many students are able to demonstrate understanding of most if not all of the concepts tested in the Boehm–3. More than 40% of all second grade students who participated in the fall standardization demonstrated knowledge of all 50 basic concepts. Because a large number of students performed perfectly during the standardization testing, the resulting percentiles were affected. Therefore, missing one or two items will make a considerable difference in the percentile score. For example, a second-grade student who was tested in the fall with *Form E* and had achieved a raw score of 49 has a percentile score of 69. This can be interpreted as the student performed as well as or better than 69% of students in his or her grade level when compared to students of the same grade level who took *Form E* in the fall. Missing one item should not be over-interpreted. It does not mean that the student needs referral for special services; it might indicate the student's inattention during that particular test item or a lack of understanding of the concept in the context that was tested. You may want to check the student's knowledge of the missed concept at a later date.

Reliability

Reliability is one of the most important psychometric characteristics of a measuring instrument. It may be considered a measure of the consistency of measurement, the accuracy of scores on the test, or the extent to which the scores are free of chance error. Measures of reliability must be of adequate magnitude to give the user confidence in the stability and precision of scores on the test that are obtained under standard conditions, and with groups for whom the test is intended. The reliability of the Boehm–3 was determined by checking internal consistency, standard error of measurement, test-retest reliability, and alternate-forms reliability.

Internal Consistency

Internal consistency reliability coefficients are used to examine the uniformity of items on a test. Boehm–3 reliability coefficients were obtained using Cronbach's coefficient alpha (Crocker & Algina, 1986). These reliability measures can be reported with a potential range from .00 to 1.00, with higher values indicating greater reliability. A test with a high level of internal consistency indicates that the internal structure of the test is such that results are repeatable. The coefficient alphas for Boehm–3 ranged from .80 to .91. As more students achieve total mastery of the concepts tested, there is less variability of performance. It can be expected that the reliability coefficients, which are dependent on variability, will decrease. The internal consistency reliability coefficients are reported in Table 4.26 by grade and form, and time of testing.

Standard Error of Measurement

An important limitation of the reliability coefficient, however is its dependency in part on the variability of the test scores from which the reliability is computed. The standard error of measurement (SEM) provides an alternate measure of reliability that is relatively independent of this variability. The SEM is an estimate of the amount of error associated with a given test score. It is used to define a band around the "true" score within which about two-thirds of the obtained raw scores would fall if a student was tested multiple times (neglecting the effects of practice, fatigue, and the like). The greater the SEM, the more variability or the greater the spread of scores present for the sample on which it was determined. The smaller the SEM, the greater the level of confidence you may have in the accuracy of the test scores. The SEM for Boehm–3 ranged from 1.14 to 2.43, indicating overall low variability. Table 4.26 reports standard error of measurements by grade, form, and time of testing.

TABLE 4.26 **Internal Consistency Reliability Coefficients (Coefficient Alpha) and Standard Error of Measurement by Grade and Form**

	Fall		Spring	
Grade	***Form E***	***Form F***	***Form E***	***Form F***
Kindergarten				
n	960	1,055	813	748
r	.90	.90	.90	.88
SEM	2.42	2.43	2.16	2.12
First Grade				
n	982	1,105	829	731
r	.85	.87	.83	.90
SEM	1.90	1.87	1.62	1.63
Second Grade				
n	924	1,029	706	717
r	.80	.80	.82	.91
SEM	1.35	1.39	1.14	1.16

Test-Retest Reliability

In a separate study, 147 kindergarten, 85 first-grade, and 81 second-grade students were administered *Form E* or *Form F* twice during fall testing to permit an analysis of the reliability of students' scores over a short time period. The sample consisted of 159 females and 154 males. The ethnicity of the sample was 16% African American, 5% Hispanic, 68% White, and 11% students of other race/ethnic groups. The participants in the study were first administered the Boehm–3 as part of the standardization study. These same students were administered the same form during a test interval of 2 to 14 days. The average retest interval was 1 week. Mean raw scores and standard deviations for test and retest are reported in Table 4.27 by form and grade. The reliability coefficients were calculated using Pearson correlation coefficients between test and retest raw scores.

TABLE 4.27 **Retest Reliability Coefficients, Means, and Standard Deviations by Form and Grade**

Form E	K	1	2	Overall
First Testing				
n	91	40	66	218
Mean	43	47	48	46
SD	5	3	2	5
Second Testing				
n	91	40	66	218
Mean	44	47	48	46
SD	5	3	2	4
	r = .80	*r* = .83	*r* = .84	*r* = .80

Form F	K	1	2	Overall
First Testing				
n	56	45	15	134
Mean	41	47	48	45
SD	8	3	2	6
Second Testing				
n	56	45	15	134
Mean	42	48	48	46
SD	6	3	2	5
	r = .88	*r* = .70	*r* = .78	*r* = .89

Alternate-Forms Reliability

Alternate form reliability is reflected in coefficients of correlation between two forms of a test. A separate study consisting of 216 first-grade students was conducted. The sample included 116 females and 110 males. The ethnic distribution of the sample was 10% African American, 4% Hispanic, 79% White, and 7% other race/ethnic groups. The study was conducted in counterbalanced order with half of the students being administered *Form E* first and half being administered *Form F* first. The test interval was 2 to 14 days, with a retest interval average of one week. Mean raw scores, standard deviations, and correlations for both forms are reported in Table 4.28 by form and grade. The reliability coefficients were calculated using Pearson correlation coefficients. It is important to note that nearly 94% of the students participating in the alternate forms study had a difference of 4 or fewer raw score points from one form to the other.

TABLE 4.28 **Alternate-Forms Reliability**

	Form E		*Form F*		
n	**Mean**	***SD***	**Mean**	***SD***	***r***
216	46.5	3.5	46.6	3.8	.83

Validity

A test can be said to have validity if it measures what it states that it measures. Evidence of Boehm–3 validity based on test content and/or relationships to other variables follows.

Evidence of Validity Based on Content

Relational concepts are used across all areas of learning in early childhood classrooms that generate language and understanding, and are used across cultures (Seigler, 1998). A sample of such relational concepts is included on Boehm–3. The content of Boehm–R is the foundation for Boehm–3. The importance of concepts assessed on the Boehm–R was re-examined in relation to the frequency of the 50 target concepts in (a) printed materials, (b) reading and mathematics curricula, and (c) teachers' verbal instructions (Boehm, Kaplan, & Preddy, 1980).

When preparing Boehm–3, more recently established word lists were sought. Little work in this area has been done since the early 1980s. A review of the Boehm–3 concepts that appeared in the *Basic Reading Vocabularies* (Harris & Jacobson, 1982) revealed that 29 of the 41 Boehm–3 *Preschool* terms in their root form were among the 500 most frequently used words across the eight reading series reviewed. The organization of the Boehm–3 *Preschool* includes 14 items that overlap with the Boehm–3, 11 of which are included in the 29 words previously mentioned. Twenty-eight of the 50 Boehm–3 words were among the 500 most frequently used words. All words were used in reading materials by second grade, except *equal, forward, match,* and *skip,* which appear in third grade reading materials; *medium-sized* appeared in fifth grade reading materials. No parallel study has been done with words that appear in mathematics materials in recent years (Ginsburg, 2000, personal communication). It is likely that words such as *equal, forward, match, skip,* and *medium-sized* might appear at earlier grade levels in mathematics materials. The terms included on the *Boehm Test of Basic Concepts* (BTBC) and its revisions were chosen based on a review of both reading and mathematics curricula.

Print Material

Although the Thorndike-Lorge list continues to be widely referenced, it is outdated and might be questioned for present day reading materials for children. A more recent study of basal reading series was conducted to establish a core vocabulary for the Educational Development Laboratories' (EDL) language arts programs (Taylor, Franckenpohl, & White, 1979). All except four of the Boehm–3 (three of the Boehm–R) terms appeared in the reading materials for kindergarten through Grade 3. (The terms that did not appear are *medium-sized, separated, equal,* and *backward.*) Based on these two sources, it can be concluded that the terms assessed by the Boehm–3 are necessary for early development of reading skills.

Curriculum Content

In view of the fact that curricular materials change over time, the original survey on which the *Boehm Test of Basic Concepts* was based (Boehm, 1967) was repeated (Boehm et al., 1980). A 20-page random sample of words to be read by the teacher or child was drawn from the workbooks of five major reading series and five major mathematics series at kindergarten, grade 1, and grade 2. All of the original Boehm terms were employed as well as synonym, antonym, and comparative forms of these terms. Results of their analyses are presented in Table 4.29. The concepts assessed by the original Boehm occurred frequently in these curricular materials, with the 50 target terms accounting for 9.5% and 8.8% of all words used on the reading and mathematics workbook pages, respectively. The Boehm terms, their antonyms and synonyms, plus easier concepts such as *in* and *under,* accounted for 30.4% and 23.7% of all the words on the reading and mathematics pages sampled, respectively. All Boehm–R terms also appeared in this sample. A new sample was not viewed as needed for Boehm–3.

TABLE 4.29 **Usage of Basic Concepts in Primary-Level Workbooks in Reading and Mathematics***

	Percentage of Total Words by Curriculum Area	
Classification of Concept	**Reading**	**Mathematics****
Concepts on BTBC, Forms A and B	9.5	8.8
Antonyms, synonyms, and comparative forms of BTBC terms	9.7	6.8
Concepts easier than those on BTBC	11.2	8.1
Total	30.4	23.7

* Based on 20-page samples drawn from each of five mathematics workbooks, at each grade level from kindergarten through grade 2. Data from Boehm, Kaplan, & Preddy (1980).

** Word counts for the mathematics materials excluded digits and other mathematical symbols.

Teacher's Verbal Instructions

The child's ability to use basic concepts is essential not only to school learning in general, but also to following teachers' verbal directions. Kaplan (1979) and Kaplan and White (1980) studied the characteristics of oral directions given by classroom teachers, as well as children's ability to follow them. An analysis of the oral directions given by 18 kindergarten through fifth-grade teachers in the Kaplan (1979) study revealed that these teachers presented directions at the rate of 1.4 per minute. The directions presented related to both academic work and classroom management. Directions consisted of behaviors to be followed such as "Sit down," and qualifiers of these behaviors such as "Sit down in the front row." The complexity of the directions used was generally stable across grades. Of the terms defined as qualifiers used by these teachers, 41% were the same as those assessed by the original Boehm. According to Kaplan and White (1980), many of the remaining qualifiers clearly resemble Boehm's relational words.

A second analysis of these transcripts for kindergarten through second-grade teachers (Boehm et al., 1980) revealed that of the 711 verbal directions presented, Boehm terms were used frequently, at a rate of .56 Boehm terms and .36 synonyms and antonyms of these terms, for a total of .92 concept terms per teacher direction (.65 Boehm–R concepts and .27 synonyms and antonyms were used per teacher direction). In addition to the use of the Boehm–3 concepts reported, teachers in these three grades frequently used easier relational concepts such as *up-down, big-little,* and *tall-short.* It can be concluded, therefore, that the basic concepts assessed by the test are used frequently in teachers' verbal directions. Furthermore, teachers often use more than one relational concept in their verbal directions. Boehm et al. (1980) analyzed the first grade transcripts from Kaplan's (1979) study to determine how teachers use basic concepts in combination. All teacher statements were considered, including brief statements such as "Okay" or "Turn to page 27." For this study, a word was counted as a basic concept if it was included on the *Boehm Test of Basic Concepts,* an antonym, synonym, or comparative form of a Boehm concept, a concept easier than those on the Boehm, or another concept such as "across," "again," or "close." The results, summarized in Table 4.30, show that of the 452 verbal statements sampled, 29.9% contained two or more relational concepts. These same concepts were included in Boehm–3.

TABLE 4.30 **Usage of Basic Concepts in the Verbal Directions of First-Grade Teachers* (*N* = 452)**

	Number of Teachers' Statements	Percent of Statements
Number of Basic Concepts	***n***	**%**
0	163	36.1
1	154	34.1
2	83	18.4
3	32	7.1
4 or more	20	4.4
Total	452	100.1

* Data from Boehm, Kaplan, & Preddy (1980).

What kinds of combinations were used? A sampling of statements includes:

> "Read the *first* sentence, Craig, in the *first* box at the *top* of the page."
>
> "Now look at the very *last pair*, 'big' and 'jig'."

These sources support the claim that the student's ability to make relational judgments using the Boehm–3 concept terms, plus their synonyms and antonyms, is basic to understanding classroom instruction, whether in the form of following teacher directions, completing curricular tasks, or reading text. Students' ability to attend to, remember, and coordinate these important components of information is essential to their use of basic concepts for thinking and in making higher-order relational decisions. Preschool teachers also use many basic concepts in their classroom talk. In a study by Boehm, Classon and Kelly (1986) in which the talk of three preschools was observed, teachers used 21 of the Boehm–3 concepts in addition to 31 concepts that are included in Boehm–3 *Preschool.* Six of these concepts overlapped the two tests. It can be surmised that students hear these concepts used in the classroom.

Evidence of Validity Based on Relationships to Other Variables

Validity evidence based on relationships to other variables was compiled in five separate studies: the relationship of Boehm–3 to Boehm–R; to *Metropolitan Achievement Tests®, Eighth Edition, Standardization Edition*; to *Metropolitan Readiness Test®, Sixth Edition*; to *Otis-Lennon School Ability Test®, Seventh Edition*; and a longitudinal study of student performance on Boehm–3, fall to spring.

Correlating Boehm–3 With Boehm–R

A study of the relationship between Boehm–3 and its predecessor, Boehm–R was conducted both in the fall and in the spring with first graders. Fifty-six students took part in the fall study and 194 students were included in the spring study. Of the students taking part in the fall study, 26 were females and 30 males, 23% African American, 18% Hispanic, 55% White, and 4% students of other race/ethnic groups. Included in the spring study were 92 females and 102 males, 3% African American, 14% Hispanic, 79% White, and 4% students of other race/ethnic groups. The tests were administered in counterbalanced order with half of the children taking either *Form E* or *Form F* of the Boehm–3 first, and half taking Boehm–R, *Form C* first. The interval between administrations was 2 to 14 days. Mean raw scores and standard deviations are reported in Table 4.31. The correlation coefficients were calculated using Pearson correlation coefficients. The correlation between these two tests ranged from .61 to .96. It is important to note that while both the Boehm–3 and its predecessor test 50 basic concepts, new concepts have been added to Boehm–3.

TABLE 4.31 **Means, Standard Deviations, and Correlations Between Boehm–3 and Boehm–R Raw Scores (*N*=250)**

	Form E				Form F			
Fall Study	*n*	**Mean**	*SD*	*r*	*n*	**Mean**	*SD*	*r*
Boehm–3	25	44.04	2.76	.96	31	44.35	3.79	.77
Boehm–R	25	42.92	6.08		31	44.35	3.35	

	Form E				Form F			
Spring Study	*n*	**Mean**	*SD*	*r*	*n*	**Mean**	*SD*	*r*
Boehm–3	95	47.37	3.94	.89	99	48.14	2.26	.61
Boehm–R	95	44.44	3.66		99	45.41	2.65	

Correlating Boehm–3 with the Metropolitan Achievement Tests®, Eighth Edition, Standardization Edition

A study was conducted to look at the relationship between Boehm–3 and the *Metropolitan Achievement Tests®, Eighth Edition* (Harcourt Educational Measurement, 1999), a test used to assess student achievement in the areas of sounds and print (emergent literacy skills), mathematics including, and language. All areas of the assessment incorporate a large number of basic concepts into the directions given to the student, and some of the actual test items in the language area test concepts such as *fewest*.

Of the 124 students taking part in the study, 69 were female, 55 were male, 6% were African American, 10% were Hispanic, 78% were White and 8% where students of other race/ethnic groups. The tests were administered in counterbalanced order with half of the students taking either Boehm–3 *Form E* or *Form F* first and half taking the MAT 8 first. The interval between administrations was 2 to 14 days. Mean raw scores and standard deviations are reported in Table 4.32. The correlation coefficients were calculated using Pearson correlation coefficients as in the previous studies. The correlation between these two tests ranged from .58 to .88, indicating that knowledge of basic concepts is important for students to comply with administration directions and performance on the test tasks.

TABLE 4.32 **Means, Standard Deviations, and Correlations Between Boehm–3 and Metropolitan Achievement Tests, Eighth Edition, (Standardization Edition) Raw Scores (*N*=124)**

		Form E				Form F			
		n	Mean	*SD*	*r*	*n*	Mean	*SD*	*r*
Boehm–3	Kindergarten	21	38.48	7.24	.88	57	38.50	8.63	.58
	First Grade	28	45.18	5.84	.79	18	46.50	4.08	.59

		Form E			Form F		
		n	Mean	*SD*	*n*	Mean	*SD*
MAT 8	Kindergarten	21	62.86	15.20	57	66.70	18.03
	First Grade	28	73.18	18.46	18	77.22	15.20

Correlating Boehm–3 with the Metropolitan Readiness Tests®, Sixth Edition

A group of 75 kindergarten students took part in a study of the relationship between Boehm–3 and the *Metropolitan Readiness Test, Sixth Edition* (Nurss & McGauvran, 1995), a group administered test of school readiness that is used to assess the early skills required in emergent reading and math. Skills tested included knowledge of beginning consonants, sound-letter correspondence, aural cloze with letter, story comprehension, and quantitative concepts and reasoning. The directions presented to the students for all portions of the test utilized a large number of basic concepts. The group was composed of 33 females and 41 males, 8% African American, 4% Hispanic, 71% White, and 17% students of other race/ethnic groups. The tests were administered in counterbalanced order with half of the students taking either Boehm–3 *Form E* or *Form F* first and half taking MRT 6 first. The interval between administrations was 2 to 14 days. Mean raw scores and standard deviations are reported in Table 4.33. The correlation coefficients were calculated using Pearson correlation coefficients. The correlations between these two tests ranged from .48 to .63.

TABLE 4.33 Means, Standard Deviations, and Correlations Between Boehm–3 and Metropolitan Readiness Tests, Sixth Edition, Raw Scores (N=75)

	Form E				Form F			
	n	Mean	*SD*	*r*	*n*	Mean	*SD*	*r*
Boehm–3	26	42.77	4.88	.63	49	41.88	4.14	.48
MRT 6	26	36.58	6.77		49	28.96	6.09	

Correlating Boehm–3 with the Otis-Lennon School Ability Test®, Seventh Edition

A large number of students in kindergarten, first, and second grades took part in a study of the relationship between Boehm–3 and the *Otis-Lennon School Ability Test* (Otis & Lennon, 1996). The OLSAT 7 is used to measure thinking and reasoning by checking student performance on tasks such as determining likenesses and differences, following directions, classifying, sequencing, completing analogies, and solving matrices. Though none of the tasks specifically target students' basic concept skills, the directions given to students to perform the tasks described earlier contain many basic concepts. The fall study included 6,173 students and the spring study included 6,756 students. The fall study was composed of 2,797 females and 2,971 males and 405 for whom no gender was reported. The ethnicity of the group included 9% African American, 15% Hispanic, 71% White, 3% students of other race/ethnic groups, and 2% for whom no race/ethnicity was reported. The spring study was composed of 3,351 females, 3,405 males, 10% African American, 8% Hispanic, 77% White, and 5% students of other race/ethnic groups. The tests were administered in counterbalanced order with half of the students taking either Boehm–3 *Form E* or *Form F* first, and the other half taking OLSAT 7 (*Level A* for kindergarten, *Level B* for first grade, and *Level C* for second grade) first. The interval between administrations was 2 to 14 days. Mean raw scores and standard deviations are reported in Table 4.34. The correlations were calculated using Pearson correlation coefficients. The correlations between these two tests ranged from .45 to .68. The moderate correlations can be expected due to the varied content of the numerous areas assessed with the OLSAT 7, suggesting that knowledge of basic concepts is strongly related to student performance and is an essential component of thinking and reasoning. This further demonstrates the need to make sure students know basic concepts prior to administering tests.

TABLE 4.34 **Means, Standard Deviations, and Correlations Between Boehm–3 and OLSAT 7 Raw Scores (*N*=12,929)**

Fall Study Boehm–3	Form E *n*	Mean	*SD*	*r*	Form F *n*	Mean	*SD*	*r*
Kindergarten	1,085	40.02	7.02	.64	913	40.29	7.03	.67
First Grade	1,027	45.72	4.32	.55	1,091	45.66	4.48	.53
Second Grade	1,103	47.93	2.40	.45	954	47.93	2.88	.48

OLSAT 7	Form E *n*	Mean	*SD*	Form F *n*	Mean	*SD*
Kindergarten	1,085	22.48	8.32	913	22.88	8.35
First Grade	1,027	24.18	8.55	1,091	24.19	8.17
Second Grade	1,103	27.54	7.23	954	27.01	7.71

Spring Study Boehm–3	Form E *n*	Mean	*SD*	*r*	Form F *n*	Mean	*SD*	*r*
Kindergarten	1,118	44.57	5.07	.68	1,076	44.89	4.33	.66
First Grade	1,221	47.28	3.12	.54	1,156	47.09	3.35	.54
Second Grade	1,093	48.73	1.71	.47	1,092	48.70	1.86	.48

OLSAT 7	Form E *n*	Mean	*SD*	Form F *n*	Mean	*SD*
Kindergarten	1,118	36.31	10.62	1,076	36.08	10.36
First Grade	1,221	35.41	10.10	1,156	35.40	10.10
Second Grade	1,093	38.57	10.36	1,092	37.93	9.05

Longitudinal Study—Fall to Spring

A group of 273 kindergarten students took part in a longitudinal study comparing their performance in the fall with their performance in the spring on the Boehm–3. Included in the study were 140 females and 133 males, 2% African American, 30% Hispanic, 67% White, and 1% students of other race/ethnic groups. Mean raw scores and standard deviations are reported in Table 4.35. The correlation coefficients were calculated using Pearson correlation coefficients. The correlation for both *Forms E* and *F* is .78, indicating that students who did well in the fall also did well in the spring.

TABLE 4.35 **Means, Standard Deviations, and Correlations for Fall to Spring Longitudinal Study (*N*=273)**

	Form E *n*	Mean	*SD*	*r*	Form F *n*	Mean	*SD*	*r*
Fall Testing	126	41.76	6.87	.78	147	42.47	7.42	.78
Spring Testing	126	37.13	7.95		147	38.33	9.00	

Summary of Research Using Boehm–3 Predecessors: *Boehm Test of Basic Concepts* and Boehm–R

The importance of the *Boehm Test of Basic Concepts* (BTBC, 1971) in relation to predicting later school achievement in kindergarten, first, and second grade has been demonstrated repeatedly (Beech 1980, 1981; Busch, 1980; Estes, Harris, Moers, & Woodrich, 1976; Nason, 1986; Piersel & McAndrews, 1982; Preddy, Boehm, & Shepherd, 1984; Steinbauer & Heller, 1978). In a more recent study using a sample of African-American urban kindergarten students, Glutting, Kelly, Boehm, & Burnett (1989) found that a fall administration of Boehm–R had moderate to substantial predictive validity of .60 with the *Metropolitan Readiness Tests* (Nurss & McGauvran, 1986). A correlation of .82 was achieved when the Boehm–R was administered in the spring and compared with performance on *The Cognitive Skills Assessment Battery*, 2nd ed. (Boehm & Slater, 1981). In addition, performance on the test was also associated with two measures of classroom behavior (Stott, McDermott, Green, & Francis, 1988a, 1988b).

The concurrent validity of the BTBC with tests of linguistic abilities has been demonstrated by Beech (1980, 1981) and Levin et al. (1975).

In order to address the question of construct validity, past factor analytic studies of the BTBC (Beech, 1980, 1981; Piersel & Reynolds, 1981) support a single factor, which Piersel and Reynolds refer to as *verbal concept acquisition*.

Instruction

Instructional activities focused on the basic concepts assessed with the BTBC have been successful in improving students' basic concept understanding and subsequent achievement at both kindergarten and preschool levels (Blai, 1973; Central Arkansas Educational Center, 1972; Levin et al., 1975; Moers & Harris, 1978; Nason, 1986; Seifert & Schwarz, 1991).

Cultural Bias

A series of studies conducted by Piersel and Reynolds (1981); Piersel, Plake, Reynolds, & Harding, (1982); and Reynolds and Piersel (1983) compared the performance of white and Mexican-American preschool and kindergarten students and that indicated cultural bias is not present in the BTBC for the sample they targeted.

Use of the *Boehm Test of Basic Concepts* With Special Populations

The overall order of difficulty of the basic concepts (assessed with the BTBC) obtained with the normative sample has been replicated in numerous studies of special populations. A tactile analogue of the BTBC (Form A), the *Tactile Test of Basic Concepts* (TTBC) was developed by Caton (1976a, b; 1977) with raised geometric forms providing the medium for the representations of pictures. The administration of the TTBC is parallel in all respects to that of the BTBC, except that it is administered individually and is preceded by five practice items. Twenty-five students who were visually impaired and attending residential and day programs were assessed at each grade level from kindergarten through second grade.

Grade placement, age, years in school, and type of school placement were all correlated with TTBC performance (.50, .28, .29, and .35, respectively). Although students who were visually impaired and enrolled in public school performed better than those in residential schools, they did not perform as well as sighted students after kindergarten, and mastery of concepts became increasingly difficult in school.

Students who are diagnosed as being developmentally delayed have significant delays in their understanding of basic concepts (Chin, 1975; Nelson & Cummings, 1981). Although these students developed concepts at a different rate from students in the normative group, there was a similar order of concept difficulty.

Students who have been classified as learning disabled also have a poorer grasp of basic concepts. Their difficulty is demonstrated both in lower mean scores and by greater variability in scores (DiNapoli, Kagedan-Kage & Boehm, 1980; Kavale, 1982).

Spector (1977) found significant differences in the performance of students who have disordered syntax compared to their non-disordered peers who had scored above the 10th percentile on the BTBC. Spector (1979) suggests that teachers and others who administer BTBC consider developing teaching strategies and stressed the importance for speech-language pathologists to develop the cognitive abilities students need to attend to, remember, and comply with directions such as those assessed by the BTBC.

Steinert (1978) found that the test serves as a general estimate of cognitive development and receptive language abilities, an outcome supported by Smith (who also standardized the test in Great Britain in 1986).

In a study by Davis (1974), children with hearing impairment did not perform as well as their age peers without hearing impairment. The degree of hearing loss was a significant factor in performance: the greater the hearing loss, the greater the difficulty on the BTBC. There was no consistent pattern of errors, underscoring what Davis referred to as the "spottiness of language concept skills" among the hearing impaired. Brown (1976) found that students who were deaf and were taught signed English were likely to acquire spatial concepts at an earlier stage than hearing impaired children taught to speechread only. Dickie (1980) found that students who were severely and profoundly hearing-impaired and were educated via the aural/oral approach, performed better on the BTBC than those educated via the total communication approach.

Non-English Versions

The BTBC and Boehm–R have been translated into a number of different languages in addition to Spanish with researchers focusing on different outcomes. Patterson (1981) found that Hutter children in South Dakota scored significantly higher on the Hutterish version of the BTBC. Mickelson and Galloway (1973) found that non-Indian children in a Canadian School scored better than Indian children. While a translated form of the test was not used in this study, the findings led the authors to conclude that Indian children may begin school with a disadvantage in the development of verbal concepts needed to deal with school learning tasks. Rosenbluth (1976) found that a Navajo translation of the test was challenging due to the more difficult syntax required in Navajo to express basic concepts. The broad range of meaning for some Navajo terms as compared to the more specific application of English terms added an additional challenge. For example, one Navajo term is used to express the basic concepts *at the top, over*, and *above*.

Zhou and Boehm (2000) found that students in Beijing, China acquired most basic concepts at an earlier age than did students in the normative group.

The findings of Rosenbluth (1976) are consistent with the work of Johnston and Slobin (1979) who studied the development of the concepts *in, on, under, beside, front*, and *back* in four languages (English, Italian, Serbo-Croatian and Turkish). Across languages, there was a general order of development of these concepts. However, both conceptual and linguistic complexities were found to interact with the development of concepts. Structural aspects of the language, such as overlapping terms or word order in a sentence, along with conceptual requirements of basic concepts terms (an object with a defined front and back, such as a chair, versus one without [e.g., a blank piece of paper]) affected the difficulty of the concepts. Johnston and Slobin suggested that relationships that can be expressed by several concepts that overlap in meaning, in contrast to one term that expresses a single meaning, might confuse students.

Chapter 5
Development and Standardization of the Spanish Edition

Developing the Test

The Spanish edition of the test was developed in conjunction with the English edition. Wording of the administration directions in Spanish or picture representations that were problematic were modified to ensure that the Spanish test items were appropriate and familiar to Spanish-speaking students.

Item Development

Most of the concepts tested in Boehm–3 have parallel words/vocabulary in English and Spanish, in which case the word conveys essentially the same meaning coded in a single word. At times, this is not the case. Look at the following.

- A word in English translates to a phrase in Spanish. For example, the word *between* in English translates to *en medio de* in Spanish.
- A word in English may not have a Spanish equivalent. For example, the concept *skip* in English had to be paired with the concept *sáltense* in Spanish. The translation of *sáltense* in English is "jump."
- Concepts are sometimes coded in different grammatical forms across languages. For instance, a locative concept coded as a preposition in English may be coded as a verb in Spanish.
- Sometimes several different concepts in English are all coded the same way in Spanish. For example, if the concepts *highest* and *top* were to be tested, only one Spanish equivalent exists for both*: más alto.*

In these situations, individuals with expertise in Spanish grammar and semantics were consulted to resolve discrepancies and make recommendations. Some of the changes recommended included altering the wording of the verbal stimuli that are presented to the student, and changes to the illustrations or the context of the item to make it more appropriate in both languages. These changes were needed to make the English and Spanish items more parallel.

Before the Boehm–3 test items were finalized for the English tryout in 1998, the items were translated by a professional Spanish translator with a broad knowledge of different Spanish dialects. Reviewers evaluated the Spanish translation of the test items to determine if they were appropriate for students who speak Spanish. Though data was not collected with Spanish-speaking students during the tryout phase of the English edition of the test, an effort was made to ensure that any of the test items selected for the English and Spanish standardization version of the test would be appropriate in both languages.

Reviewers were asked to determine whether the translation of each test item represented appropriate use of the concept word in Spanish. The English and Spanish languages do not necessarily use the same concept to express certain relationships between objects. For example, if testing the concept *up*, it is best to avoid a picture of a person climbing up a ladder or tree. While in English we can climb up or climb down, in Spanish the context requires the use of *subir* (climb up) or *bajar* (climb down) instead of a separate preposition such as *up* or *down*. In addition to determining whether the concept was used in an appropriate context, reviewers evaluated the appropriateness of the vocabulary for the different dialects in Spanish, and the familiarity of the situations depicted in the art for Spanish-speaking students.

Multiple individuals with training in translations and in Spanish grammar reviewed the tryout item set to ensure that the translation was grammatically correct.

The reviewers, who all are experts in Spanish-language issues and multicultural assessment, included:

José Ramón de la Fuente
Bilingual Speech and Language Pathologist and Diagnostician
Weld County School District #6
Greely, Colorado

Henriette W. Langdon
Associate Professor
San José State University
San José, California

E. Judith Riggin
Bilingual Speech and Language Pathologist
Yakima, Washington

Albert Villanueva-Reyes
Director del Programa de Patologia del Habla y Lenguaje
Universidad de Puerto Rico
Mayaguez, Puerto Rico

Standardization Testing

National fall norms for the Spanish version of Boehm–3 were developed by administering *Forms E* and *F* to students in kindergarten, first, and second grade in October and November of 1999. Spring standardization took place in April and May of 2000. Bilingual teachers who were experienced in test administration were invited to participate in the standardization testing.

Description of the Fall and Spring Samples

More than 1,200 Spanish-speaking students in the United States participated in the fall standardization and the related reliability and validity studies of the Boehm–3 Spanish edition. More than 400 Spanish-speaking students participated in the spring standardization and validity studies. Some of the tests received were excluded from the standardization studies due to missing information. School districts and non-public schools from around the country were invited to participate; however, little or no response was received from some areas of the country, particularly the Northeast, despite heavy recruiting Tables 5.1 through 5.5 report the demographic characteristics of the Spanish fall and spring samples.

Table 5.1 reports the number of students in each grade for which norms are reported by form, fall and spring.

TABLE 5.1 **Boehm–3 Spanish Standardization Sample by Grade and Form—Fall and Spring**

	Fall				Spring			
	Form E		*Form F*		*Form E*		*Form F*	
Grade	*n*	%	*n*	%	*n*	%	*n*	%
K	144	41.0	140	31.0	85	49.7	20	15.9
1	121	35.0	147	32.0	42	24.6	58	46.0
2	82	24.0	171	37.0	44	25.7	48	38.1
Total	347	100.0	458	100.0	171	100.0	126	100.0

Table 5.2 shows the distribution of the Spanish standardization sample by gender and form, fall and spring.

TABLE 5.2 **Boehm–3 Spanish Standardization Sample by Gender and Form—Fall and Spring**

	Fall				Spring			
	Form E		*Form F*		*Form E*		*Form F*	
Gender	*n*	%	*n*	%	*n*	%	*n*	%
Male	189	54.5	237	51.7	87	50.9	55	43.7
Female	158	45.5	221	48.3	84	49.1	71	56.3
Total	347	100.0	458	100.0	171	100.0	126	100.0

Table 5.3 shows the geographical distribution of students participating in the Boehm–3 Spanish standardization by form, fall and spring. You will notice that the sample consists of students from those regions of the United States that typically have a large population of students who are Spanish speakers.

TABLE 5.3 **Boehm–3 Spanish Standardization Sample by Region and Form—Fall and Spring**

	Fall				Spring			
	Form E		*Form F*		*Form E*		*Form F*	
Region	*n*	%	*n*	%	*n*	%	*n*	%
Northeast	—	—	29	6.3	—	—	—	—
South	159	45.8	245	53.5	108	63.2	90	71.4
West	188	54.2	184	40.2	63	36.8	36	28.6
Total	347	100.0	458	100.0	171	100.0	126	100.0

School districts participating in the standardization study were characterized by the socioeconomic level of the district. There were three levels: low, middle, and high. The levels were determined by reviewing the income level and education of residents within a defined school district. These classifications were designed to place 33% of the public school district population into each of the three categories. This index was provided using the *1992–93 National Center for Educational Statistics Public Agency data tape.* Students participating in the standardization study who attend non-public schools were included as a fourth category. Table 5.4 reports the distribution of school districts and non-public schools included in the study by form, fall and spring.

TABLE 5.4 **Boehm–3 Spanish Standardization Sample by Socioeconomic Level of the School District and Non-public Schools and Form—Fall and Spring**

	Fall				Spring			
	Form E		*Form F*		*Form E*		*Form F*	
Socioeconomic Level	*n*	%	*n*	%	*n*	%	*n*	%
Low	101	29.1	117	25.5	21	12.3	16	12.7
Middle	159	45.8	245	53.5	76	44.4	75	59.5
High	5	1.4	12	2.6	74	43.3	35	27.8
Non-public	82	23.6	84	18.3	—	—	—	—
Total	347	100.0	458	100.0	171	100.0	126	100.0

Table 5.5 demonstrates the urbanicity of the school districts and non-public schools that were included in the Spanish standardization study. Urbanicity can be defined as the school district's service area relative to the Metropolitan Service Area and is based on zip code information of the district. There are three primary levels of urbanicity: urban, suburban, and rural. This information was obtained from the *1990–91 National Center for Educational Statistics Public Agency data tape.* The percentage of students participating from non-public schools is also included.

TABLE 5.5 **Boehm–3 Spanish Standardization Sample by Urbanicity and Form—Fall and Spring**

	Fall				Spring			
	Form E		*Form F*		*Form E*		*Form F*	
Urbanicity	*n*	%	*n*	%	*n*	%	*n*	%
Urban	57	16.4	39	8.5	35	20.5	16	12.7
Suburban	159	45.8	245	53.5	67	39.2	54	42.9
Rural	49	14.1	90	19.7	69	40.4	56	44.4
Non-public	82	23.6	84	18.3	—	—	—	—
Total	347	100.0	458	100.0	171	100.0	126	100.0

Developing Norms

A large, representative sample of Spanish-speaking students took either *Form E* or *Form F*. Both forms tested the same concepts in the same order with different contexts. The item *p*-values (percent correct) were used to look at item progression and compare the parallel test items across both forms. The percent of student responding correctly was analyzed by grade and by a combination of the three grades. Item progression from grade to grade was also assessed. In addition, item difficulties and item-total correlations were examined. Based on the data and in coordination with the English edition of the test, the same five items were deleted to bring the total number of items to 50 per form.

Table 5.6 depicts the percent of students passing each item by grade and time of testing for *Form E*. Table 5.7 depicts these items for *Form F*.

As noted in an earlier section, you will notice that several concepts that were administered to the Spanish-speaking students did not follow a typical progression across grades. One explanation may be that some second-grade students are more immersed in English and may have forgotten some of the concepts in Spanish. It is also possible that in English these concepts are more concrete, while in Spanish, the concept is relative to the proximity of a person or location. For example, *next* in Spanish relates to the closeness or proximity of one object or person to another. While this is true in some contexts in English, it is not universally true. In addition, some concepts in Spanish may have more than one meaning. For example, the Spanish word *sobre* can reflect both the prepositions *over* and *on*.

TABLE 5.6 **Percent of Students Passing Each Item, *Form E*, (*N* = 347 Students in the Fall Standardization and *N* = 171 Students in the Spring Standardization)**

		Fall			Spring		
Item	**Concept**	**K**	**1**	**2**	**K**	**1**	**2**
1	Más alto	89	98	96	98	98	95
2	El centro	72	77	85	72	67	91
3	Completo(a)	78	96	99	93	98	95
4	Al lado	69	83	95	81	95	95
5	Último	65	93	98	76	100	98
6	Mediano	61	69	93	58	79	93
7	Siempre	87	99	100	94	100	98
8	Derecha	40	53	55	39	48	57
9	Esquina	70	93	96	81	93	89
10	Antes	40	59	71	29	64	73
11	Final	64	83	92	55	93	93
12	Más lejos	77	96	100	89	93	93
13	Parte	57	79	89	53	86	80
14	A través	92	98	98	98	100	89
15	Algunos(as)	49	55	74	44	50	59
16	Arriba	96	100	99	99	100	100
17	Separados(as)	60	86	98	71	90	91
18	Primer	85	94	100	86	100	98
19	Línea	90	98	100	96	100	98
20	Pocos(as)	83	93	99	92	95	98
21	Más cerca	26	61	85	58	57	70
22	Cada	67	70	72	24	64	80
23	Más abajo	90	89	89	94	90	100
24	Nunca	75	86	95	49	88	91
25	Empezando	33	55	80	18	57	59
26	Segundo	28	55	91	35	83	86
27	En frente	88	97	94	87	100	100
28	Más ancha	65	78	73	68	71	82
29	Retirado	65	79	93	67	81	82
30	Mitad	65	69	93	54	86	91
31	Iguales	94	97	99	98	100	95
32	La menor cantidad	35	42	39	21	38	27
33	Hacen juego	64	73	85	52	64	70
34	Sobre	85	87	74	78	79	84
35	Tantos . . . como	73	84	93	78	95	84
36	Tercer(a)	24	59	89	41	79	100
37	Otro	42	62	72	47	81	66
38	Empezando	92	97	96	86	98	100
39	Más	69	83	100	73	95	86
40	Detrás	90	97	40	99	100	98
41	Izquierda	35	51	96	31	29	27
42	En medio de	72	83	99	76	81	89
43	Diferente	80	93	94	82	95	98
44	Par	70	86	99	56	90	95
45	Debajo	97	99	91	96	98	100
46	Sáltense	48	36	54	5	10	7
47	Inclinado(a)	35	48	78	20	26	23
48	Menos	55	77	81	71	88	75
49	Hacia atrás	30	42	85	12	43	43
50	Igual	50	73	93	51	81	89
n		144	121	82	21	76	74

TABLE 5.7 Percent of Students Passing Each Item, *Form F*, (*N* = 458 Students in the Fall Standardization and *N* = 126 Students in the Spring Standardization)

		Fall			Spring		
Item	Concept	K	1	2	K	1	2
1	Más alto	54	68	84	55	76	79
2	El centro	59	67	81	95	76	88
3	Completo	63	84	94	75	95	94
4	Al lado	65	82	95	90	97	98
5	Último	63	88	98	95	93	100
6	Mediano	42	63	84	70	81	92
7	Siempre	86	97	99	100	100	100
8	Derecha	16	22	49	10	36	46
9	Esquina	46	79	88	80	84	92
10	Antes	48	67	75	50	71	85
11	Final	45	60	88	85	86	96
12	Más lejos	60	86	92	90	91	100
13	Parte	54	80	88	85	90	92
14	A través	84	93	96	95	95	100
15	Algunos(as)	39	42	67	50	62	71
16	Arriba	91	97	98	95	95	100
17	Separados(as)	55	78	91	85	88	96
18	Primer	79	92	97	100	95	98
19	Línea	83	93	99	95	98	100
20	Pocos(as)	72	83	95	95	100	100
21	Más cerca	29	53	81	60	62	73
22	Cada	64	59	71	35	74	90
23	Más abajo	80	95	97	90	98	96
24	Nunca	41	64	89	70	86	88
25	Empezando	59	73	88	70	83	94
26	Segundo	23	54	82	80	79	92
27	En frente	87	95	99	100	100	100
28	Más ancha	66	70	76	75	79	90
29	Retirado	66	84	92	90	88	96
30	Mitad	51	68	86	60	88	90
31	Iguales	79	93	98	85	97	98
32	La menor cantidad	33	33	54	55	74	50
33	Hacen juego	54	63	77	85	88	73
34	Sobre	75	82	91	85	84	98
35	Tantos . . . como	65	77	82	75	93	94
36	Tercer(a)	15	35	77	55	76	88
37	Otro	46	70	92	75	88	90
38	Empezando	81	89	91	95	97	98
39	Más	91	99	99	95	95	96
40	Detrás	31	29	51	100	100	98
41	Izquierda	71	80	94	45	43	35
42	En medio de	81	94	98	80	86	96
43	Diferente	34	51	75	90	98	100
44	Par	95	99	100	65	64	88
45	Debajo	13	10	52	95	100	100
46	Sáltense	18	17	50	30	24	54
47	Inclinado(a)	53	66	76	45	26	46
48	Menos	30	35	61	50	66	77
49	Hacia atrás	44	81	89	65	57	63
50	Igual	73	86	91	60	91	92
n		140	147	171	16	75	35

Raw Scores

A raw score is the total number of items the student answered correctly. Table 5.8 reports mean raw scores and standard deviations for standardization by form and grade, fall and spring. Mean raw scores increase across the three grades (K, 1, and 2) demonstrating the increase in understanding of basic concepts over time. A decrease in the standard deviation over time demonstrates that there is less variability of scores as students acquire understanding of basic concepts. Because of the variation among sample sizes, differences in means and standard deviations may be noted.

TABLE 5.8 **Boehm–3 Spanish Standardization Sample Mean Raw Scores and Standard Deviations by Grade and Form (Fall *N* = 347 for *Form E*, *N* = 458 for *Form F*; Spring *N* = 171 for *Form E*, *N* = 126 for *Form F***

	Fall		Spring	
Grade	***Form E***	***Form F***	***Form E***	***Form F***
Kindergarten				
n	144	140	85	20
mean	32.46	28.47	32.29	37.55
SD	8.00	8.45	5.97	6.56
First Grade				
n	121	147	42	58
mean	39.02	35.21	39.95	40.93
SD	6.76	6.48	5.32	5.44
Second Grade				
n	82	171	44	48
mean	42.79	42.18	40.80	43.63
SD	4.63	6.15	5.24	4.63

Percent Correct

The percent correct is the score that indicates the percentage of items that the student answered correctly. For example, if the student received a raw score of 49 the percent correct would be 98. Table 5.9 contains the raw score and corresponding percent correct irrespective of form, grade, language of administration, or time of testing. Alternatively, this calculation can be completed easily by doubling the raw score (because a total of 50 items were presented) to determine the percent correct.

TABLE 5.9 **Percent Correct for All Grades (K, 1, 2), *Forms E* and *F***

Raw Score	% Correct	Raw Score	% Correct
50	100	25	50
49	98	24	48
48	96	23	46
47	94	22	44
46	92	21	42
45	90	20	40
44	88	19	38
43	86	18	36
42	84	17	34
41	82	16	32
40	80	15	30
39	78	14	28
38	76	13	26
37	74	12	24
36	72	11	22
35	70	10	20
34	68	9	18
33	66	8	16
32	64	7	14
31	62	6	12
30	60	5	10
29	58	4	8
28	56	3	6
27	54	2	4
26	52	1	2

Performance Range

Because no precision would be gained by examining the standardization data in smaller units, it was determined that student performance could be best described using three ranges; the upper third, middle third and lower third. Use of a performance range makes it easier for parents to understand their child's performance in relation to his or her grade level peers. To determine the appropriate performance range, locate the appropriate time of testing, then find the student's grade. Locate the form of the test that was administered. Using the student's raw score, locate the appropriate performance range. A performance range of *1* means that the student knows the basic concepts needed to perform at grade level. A performance range of *2* means the student knows most of the basic concepts, but lacks understanding of some key concepts. A performance range of *3* means that the student's knowledge of basic concepts is extremely low and teacher and parent help is needed for the childs success in school. Table 5.10 provides the performance ranges by form and grade, fall and spring.

TABLE 5.10 **Boehm–3 Spanish Fall Standardization Edition Performance Ranges by Form and Grade—Fall and Spring**

	Fall		Spring	
Kindergarten Performance Range	***Form E* Raw Scores**	***Form F* Raw Scores**	***Form E* Raw Scores**	***Form F* Raw Scores**
1	37–50	33–50	34–50	42–50
2	30–36	24–32	29–33	36–41
3	1–29	1–23	1–28	1–35
First Grade Performance Range	***Form E* Raw Scores**	***Form F* Raw Scores**	***Form E* Raw Scores**	***Form F* Raw Scores**
1	43–50	39–50	43–50	45–50
2	37–42	34–38	38–42	39–44
3	1–36	1–33	1–37	1–38
Second Grade Performance Range	***Form E* Raw Scores**	***Form F* Raw Scores**	***Form E* Raw Scores**	***Form F* Raw Scores**
1	46–50	46–50	43–50	46–50
2	43–45	41–45	41–42	42–45
3	1–42	1–40	1–40	1–41

Percentile Score

Percentile norms corresponding to Boehm–3 Spanish edition raw scores are presented in Tables 5.11 and 5.12. Table 5.11 shows the raw scores and percentiles for students tested with *Form E*, fall and spring. Table 5.12 shows the raw scores and percentiles for students tested with *Form F*, fall and spring.

The percentile score is determined by locating the student's raw score in the left column and looking at the appropriate time of testing, find the corresponding percentile score in the appropriate grade column. When reviewing a student's percentile score, the percentile should be interpreted as "the student performed as well as or better than ___% of his or her grade-level peers in the standardization sample who took the same form of Boehm–3 Spanish."

TABLE 5.11 Boehm–3 Spanish Percentile by Grade for *Form E* (*N*=347 for Fall Testing and *N*=171 for Spring Testing)

	Fall Percentile			Spring Percentile		
Raw Score	**K**	**1**	**2**	**K**	**1**	**2**
50	>99	>99	99	>99	>99	>99
49	99	99	98	>99	>99	>99
48	98	94	96	>99	>99	>99
47	97	86	90	99	97	95
46	96	85	79	99	97	93
45	95	75	71	98	95	88
44	94	74	59	97	83	74
43	93	72	46	96	71	70
42	90	66	34	95	63	57
41	86	60	24	92	54	44
40	80	55	20	90	45	31
39	77	52	18	87	38	24
38	72	43	17	83	33	22
37	70	38	12	76	23	15
36	66	33	8	74	19	13
35	61	28	7	71	16	11
34	59	23	5	67	14	11
33	53	19	5	59	13	10
32	48	15	5	51	11	8
31	43	12	4	47	10	6
30	38	8	3	42	8	4
29	35	7	2	38	7	4
28	31	6	<1	31	4	<1
27	24	5	<1	19	4	<1
26	22	4	<1	14	4	<1
25	21	3	<1	8	4	<1
24	18	2	<1	8	4	<1
23	16	1	<1	7	4	<1
22	10	1	<1	5	2	<1
21	6	1	<1	3	<1	<1
20	4	1	<1	3	<1	<1
19	4	1	<1	1	<1	<1
18	3	<1	<1	<1	<1	<1
17	2	<1	<1	<1	<1	<1
16	2	<1	<1	<1	<1	<1
15	2	<1	<1	<1	<1	<1
14	2	<1	<1	<1	<1	<1
13	1	<1	<1	<1	<1	<1
12	1	<1	<1	<1	<1	<1
11	1	<1	<1	<1	<1	<1
10 or less	<1	<1	<1	<1	<1	<1

TABLE 5.12 Boehm–3 Spanish Percentile by Grade for *Form F* (*N*=458 for Fall Testing and *N*=126 for Spring Testing)

	Fall Percentile			Spring Percentile		
Raw Score	K	1	2	K	1	2
50	>99	>99	99	>99	>99	>99
49	>99	>99	94	>99	>99	93
48	>99	99	90	>99	>99	89
47	>99	98	83	>99	94	85
46	>99	97	74	89	87	68
45	99	95	65	89	79	58
44	97	93	59	85	65	49
43	95	90	50	85	56	41
42	93	87	44	84	48	33
41	91	82	37	60	48	22
40	89	78	33	59	43	20
39	87	73	26	55	36	14
38	85	65	22	54	29	12
37	83	59	16	49	27	10
36	79	55	14	44	22	10
35	77	50	11	29	20	8
34	74	44	8	25	15	8
33	70	41	7	25	10	4
32	67	31	5	24	6	4
31	64	27	4	19	5	4
30	59	20	2	14	3	4
29	54	16	2	14	3	4
28	50	14	2	10	3	1
27	47	12	2	10	3	<1
26	40	9	2	9	3	<1
25	39	6	2	5	3	<1
24	34	6	2	4	1	<1
23	32	5	1	<1	<1	<1
22	26	4	1	<1	<1	<1
21	22	3	1	<1	<1	<1
20	18	2	<1	<1	<1	<1
19	16	2	<1	<1	<1	<1
18	12	1	<1	<1	<1	<1
17	9	1	<1	<1	<1	<1
16	7	<1	<1	<1	<1	<1
15	6	<1	<1	<1	<1	<1
14	3	<1	<1	<1	<1	<1
13	2	<1	<1	<1	<1	<1
12	1	<1	<1	<1	<1	<1
11 or less	<1	<1	<1	<1	<1	<1

Reliability

Reliability is one of the most important psychometric characteristics of a measuring instrument. It may be considered a measure of the consistency of measurement, the accuracy of scores on the test, or the extent to which the scores are free of chance error. Measures of reliability must be of adequate magnitude to give the user confidence in the stability and precision of scores on the test that are obtained under standard conditions, and with groups for whom the test is intended. The reliability of the Boehm–3 Spanish edition was determined by checking internal consistency, standard error of measurement, and test-retest reliability.

Internal Consistency

Internal consistency reliability coefficients are used to examine the uniformity of items on a test. Boehm–3 Spanish edition reliability coefficients were obtained using Cronbach's coefficient alpha (Crocker & Algina, 1986), following the same procedure as had been used in the English edition. These reliability measures can be reported with a potential range of from .00 to 1.00, with higher values indicating greater reliability. A test with a high level of internal consistency indicates that the internal structure of the test is such that results are repeatable. The coefficient alphas for Boehm–3 Spanish edition ranged from .79 to .88. The internal consistency reliability coefficients are reported in Table 5.13. They are presented by form and grade, fall and spring.

Standard Error of Measurement

An important limitation of the reliability coefficient, however, it its dependency in part on the variability of the test scores from which the reliability is computed. The standard error of measurement (SEM) provides an alternate measure of reliability that is relatively independent of this variability. The SEM is an estimate of the amount of error associated with a given test score. It is used to define a band around the "true" score within which about two-thirds of the obtained raw scores would fall if a student was tested multiple times (neglecting the effects of practice, fatigue, and the like). The greater the SEM, the more variability or the greater the spread of scores is present for the sample on which it was determined. The smaller the SEM, the greater the level of confidence you may have in the accuracy of the test scores. The SEM for the Boehm–3 Spanish edition ranged from 2.02 to 2.90 indicating overall low variability. Table 5.13 reports standard error of measurement by form and grade, fall and spring.

TABLE 5.13 **Boehm–3 Spanish Internal Consistency Reliability Coefficients (Coefficient Alpha) and Standard Error of Measurement by Grade and Form—Fall and Spring**

Grade	Fall Form E	Fall Form F	Spring Form E	Spring Form F
Kindergarten				
n	144	140	85	20
r	.87	.88	.79	.84
SEM	2.88	2.90	2.74	2.62
First Grade				
n	121	147	42	58
r	.86	.83	.81	.82
SEM	2.52	2.67	2.32	2.31
Second Grade				
n	82	171	44	48
r	.79	.87	.83	.81
SEM	2.12	2.21	2.16	2.02

Test-Retest Reliability

In a separate study, 106 students from a combined group of kindergarten, first and second graders were administered *Form E* or *Form F* twice during fall testing to permit an analysis of the reliability of students' scores over a short time period. The sample consisted of 50 females and 56 males, all of whom were Spanish-speakers. The participants in the study were first administered the Boehm–3 Spanish edition as part of the standardization study. These same students were administered the same form during a test interval of 2 to 14 days. The average retest interval was 1 week. The reliability coefficients were calculated using Pearson correlation coefficients between test and retest raw scores. The correlations ranged from .78 to .80. Mean raw scores and standard deviations for test and retest are reported in Table 5.14 by form.

TABLE 5.14 **Boehm–3 Spanish Retest Reliability Coefficients, Means, and Standard Deviations by Form**

	Form E	Form F
First Testing		
n	64	42
Mean	35	43
SD	6	6
Second Testing		
n	64	42
Mean	35	43
SD	7	6
	r = .80	*r* = .78

Validity

A test can be said to have validity if it measures what it states it measures. Evidence based on relationships to other variables is addressed here.

Correlating Boehm–3 Spanish Edition With the Naglieri Nonverbal Ability Test®

A study was conducted in the fall to look at the relationship between the Boehm–3 Spanish edition and the *Naglieri Nonverbal Ability Test* (NNAT, 1996) a group-administered test that is used to measure general ability. The student is required to solve a problem with all of the necessary information provided for them. The student's use of reasoning and problem solving skills are assessed. Of the 338 Spanish-speaking students taking part in the study, 163 were female and 175 were male. The tests were administered in counterbalanced order with half of the students taking either *Form E* or *Form F* of the Boehm–3 Spanish edition first (these students were included in the standardization study) and half taking the NNAT first (these students were excluded from the standardization study). The interval between administrations was 2 to 14 days. Mean raw scores and standard deviations are reported in Table 5.15. The correlations were calculated using Pearson correlation coefficients. The correlations between these two tests range from .32 to .59 indicating that the NNAT is measuring more than basic concepts, but understanding basic concepts is related to problem solving.

TABLE 5.15 **Means, Standard Deviations, and Correlations Between Boehm–3 and Naglieri Nonverbal Ability Test (*N*=338)**

	Form E				Form F			
Boehm–3	***n***	**Mean**	***SD***	***r***	***n***	**Mean**	***SD***	***r***
Kindergarten	63	36.51	7.53	.48	47	32.70	9.90	.59
First Grade	38	44.68	4.59	.54	75	35.73	7.58	.55
Second Grade	38	44.97	3.28	.32	77	43.62	5.40	.43

	Form E			Form F		
NNAT	***n***	**Mean**	***SD***	***n***	**Mean**	***SD***
Kindergarten	63	24.16	10.86	47	20.60	8.08
First Grade	38	33.24	9.39	75	20.77	10.51
Second Grade	38	26.70	10.85	77	26.67	9.86

Appendix A

Percent Passing Table

Number of Students Answering Item Correctly	Number of Students Tested 11	12	13	14	15	16	17	18	19	20	21	22	23	24	25	26	27	28	29	30
0	0	0	0	0	0	0	0	0	0	0	0	0	0	0	0	0	0	0	0	0
1	9	8	8	7	7	6	6	6	5	5	5	5	4	4	4	4	4	4	3	3
2	18	17	15	14	13	12	12	11	11	10	10	9	9	8	8	8	7	7	7	7
3	27	25	23	21	20	19	18	17	16	15	14	14	13	12	12	12	11	11	10	10
4	36	33	31	29	27	25	24	22	21	20	19	18	17	17	16	15	15	14	14	13
5	45	42	38	36	33	31	29	28	26	25	24	23	22	21	20	19	19	18	17	17
6	55	50	46	43	40	38	35	33	32	30	29	27	26	25	24	23	22	21	21	20
7	64	58	54	50	47	44	41	39	37	35	33	32	30	29	28	27	26	25	24	23
8	73	67	62	57	53	50	47	44	42	40	38	36	35	33	32	31	30	29	28	27
9	82	75	69	64	60	56	53	50	47	45	43	41	39	38	36	35	33	32	31	30
10	91	83	77	71	67	62	59	56	53	50	48	45	43	42	40	38	37	36	34	33
11	100	92	85	79	73	69	65	61	58	55	52	50	48	46	44	42	41	39	38	37
12		100	92	86	80	75	71	67	63	60	57	55	52	50	48	46	44	43	41	40
13			100	93	87	81	76	72	68	65	62	59	57	54	52	50	48	46	45	43
14				100	93	88	82	78	74	70	67	64	61	58	56	54	52	50	48	47
15					100	94	88	83	79	75	71	68	65	62	60	58	56	54	52	50
16						100	94	89	84	80	76	73	70	67	64	62	59	57	55	53
17							100	94	89	85	81	77	74	71	68	65	63	61	59	57
18								100	95	90	86	82	78	75	72	69	67	64	62	60
19									100	95	90	86	83	79	76	73	70	68	66	64
20										100	95	91	87	83	80	77	74	71	69	67
21											100	95	91	88	84	81	78	75	72	70
22												100	96	92	88	85	81	79	76	73
23													100	96	92	88	85	82	79	77
24														100	96	92	89	86	83	80
25															100	96	93	89	86	83
26																100	96	93	90	87
27																	100	96	93	90
28																		100	97	93
29																			100	97
30																				100

DIRECTIONS: Locate the appropriate column for the number of students tested. Locate the number of students answering the item correctly (at the far left of the table). Move across this row to the appropriate column to find the percent passing the item. For example, if 17 out of a class of 22 students answer a certain item correctly, the percent passing the item is read as 77.

Appendix B

Schools Participating in Boehm–3 Tryout Testing

Schools	City and State
Akron Public Schools	Akron, OH
Allen Bowden School District	Tulsa, OK
Altoona Area School District	Altoona, PA
Avon School District	Avon, MT
Bethany Christian School	Brevard, NC
Big Jackson School District	Paris, MI
Bonner School District	Bonner, MT
Briggs Elementary School District	Santa Paula, CA
Bullitt County	Bullitt, CO
Butler County	Greenville, AL
Canton Public School District	Canton, MS
Carbon Cliff-Barston	Carbon Cliff, IL
Christ Crusader Academy	New York, NY
Dodge Public Schools	Dodge, ND
Dolton School District 148	Riverdale, IL
Essex North SAU	Canaan, VT
Flowing Wells School District	Tucson, AZ
Ft. Wayne Community Schools	Ft. Wayne, IN
Huntsville City School	Huntsville, AL
Isle au Haut	Isle au Haut, ME
Jessamine County	Nicholasville, KY
Lawrence School District	Lawrence, MA
Lostant School District #425	Lostant, IL
Mark Twain R-8	Rueter, MO
MCCA	Hookerton, NC
Nadaburg School District #81	Wittmann, AZ
Nedrose School District	Minot, ND
Nell Holcomb R-IV	Cape Girardeau, MO
Newport Independent	Newport, KY
Orange East Supervisory Union	Thetford, VT
Our Lady of Perpetual Help	Dallas, TX
Placer Hills Union School District	Meadow Vista, CA
Prairieview District 192	Royal, IL
Reed City Public Schools	Reed City, MI
Resurrection Catholic Elementary	Pascagoula, MS
Richland/Lerdo	Shafter, CA
SAD #31	Enfield, ME
SAU #16	Newfields, NH
Sauk Rapids #47	Sauk Rapids, MN
St. Peter Lutheran School	Joliet, IL
St. Phillips School	Bemidji, MN
Sunrise School District	Desoto, MO
Texarkana I.S.D.	Texarkana, AR
Vysehrad I.S.D	Hallettsville, TX
Wekowa School District #54	Wewoka, OK
White Rock School District	McLoud, OK
Whitmore Union Elementary	Whitmore, CA
Worcester	Still River, MA

Appendix C

Schools Participating in Boehm–3 Standardization Testing

Fall

Schools	City and State
Altoona School District	Altoona, PA
American Christian Academy	Northport, AL
Archdiocese of Mobile	Mobile, AL
Archdiocese of St. Paul	Saint Paul, MN
Bandon Pacific Christian School	Bandon, OR
Beach Park School District	Beach Park, IL
Bellingham Public School District	Bellingham, MA
Blue Ridge Independent School District	Blue Ridge, TX
Canastota Central School District	Canastota, NY
Central Baptist Schools	Texarkana, AR
Clinton Independent School District	Clinton, OK
Currier Memorial School District	Danby, VT
Diocese of Brownsville	Alamo, TX
Diocese of Fresno	Fresno, CA
Diocese of Galveston	Galveston, TX
Diocese of Houston	Houston, TX
Diocese of Kansas City	Kansas City, MO
District 5L	Plainview, NE
Douglas School District	Douglas, MA
Early Independent School District	Early, TX
Fairport Harbor School District	Fairport Harbor, OH
Farmington School District	Farmington, NH
Fayetteville School District	Fayetteville, AR
Finneytown School District	Finneytown, OH
Gadsden City School District	Gadsden, AL
Genoa Central School District	Texarkana, AR
Greene County School District	Greene County, VA
Heritage Academy Elementary School	Columbus, MS
Huntley Project School District	Worden, MT
Island Trees Public School District	Livittown, NY
Justice School District 54	Wewoka, OK
Keystone Public School District	Keystone, OK
Kingwood Christian School	Alabaster, AL
Lansing School District	Lansing, MI
Laona School District	Laona, WI
Liberty Academy	Shawnee, OK
Lordsburg School District	Lordsburg, NM
Manatee County Schools	Bredenton, FL
Marion County School District	Everton, AR
Marion County School District	Fairmont, WV
Martin County School District	Martin County, KY
McKittrick School District	McKittrick, CA
Middlesboro Independent School District	Middleboro, KY
Millwood Independent School District	Oklahoma City, OK
Maine School Administrative District 14	Weston, ME
Maine School Administrative District 59	Madison, ME
Maine School Administrative District 76	Bar Harbor, ME
Mountain View School District	Kingsley, PA
New World Educational Center	Phoenix, AZ
North Wamac Grade School #186	Centralia, IL

Orchard Prairie School District	Spokane, WA
Page Private School	Los Angeles, CA
Piedmont City School District	Piedmont, AL
Pike County School District	Pikeville, KY
Ravenswood City Elementary School	East Palo Alto, CA
Red River Parish School District	Hall Summit, LA
Roseville City School District	Roseville, CA
Sarasota County Schools	Sarasota, FL
Savannah R V School District	Savannah, MO
Shawnee School District	Lima, OH
Shelbyville School District 4	Shelbyville, IL
Socorro Independent School District	El Paso, TX
Springfield Public School District	Springfield, MA
St. Mark Lutheran School	Watertown, WI
Standish Sterling Community School	Standish, MI
Taliaferro School District	Crawfordville, GA
Texarkana School District 7	Texarkana, AR
Union District	Danby, VT
Union District	Manchester, VT
Walnut Grove School District R	Walnut Grove, MO
Watertown School District	Watertown, AR
Weiner Public School District	Weiner, AR
West Fresno School District	Fresno, CA
West Washington School District	Campbellsburg, IN
Westside Elementary School District	Five Points, CA
Wewoka District D-54	Wewoka, OK
White Rock School District	McLoud, OK
Wing Public School District #28	Wing, ND
Woodland School District	Woodland, ME
Zion Lutheran School	Plainview, NE

Schools Participating in Boehm–3 Standardization Testing

Spring

Schools	City and State
Antioch Community Consolidated School District 34	Antioch, IL
Arcata Christian School	Arcata, CA
Bandon Pacific Christian School	Bandon, OR
Blue Ridge Independent School District	Blue Ridge, TX
Botetourt County School District	Blue Ridge, VA
Bryant Public School District	Bryant, AR
Calvary Christian School	Fairmont, WV
Carrizozo Municipal School District	Carrizozo, NM
Cedar Park Christian School	Bothell, WA
Cedarville Public School District	Cedarville, AR
Charleston Public School District	Charleston, AR
Corsicana Independent School District	Corsicana, TX

Crusaders for Christ Christian Academy	Philadelphia, PA
Cumberland Christian School	Vineland, NJ
Currier Memorial School District	Danby, VT
Decatur Public School District	Decatur, AR
Deer Park Independent School District	Deer Park, TX
Derby School District	Derby, CT
Dickson County School District	Dickson, TN
Diocese of Dallas Schools	Dallas, TX
Diocese of Galveston-Houston Schools	Houston, TX
Diocese of Norwich Schools	Middletown, CT
Diocese of Pittsburgh Schools	Pittsburgh, PA
Diocese of Tucson Schools	Tucson, AZ
Duncan Independent School District I-1	Duncan, OK
Eagle Seventh Day Adventist School	Eagle, ID
Jackson County District	Jackson County, MS
Edison Elementary School District	Bakersfield, CA
Elsberry School District R-2	Elsberry, MO
Evangel Christian School	Long Island City, NY
Fairmont Private Schools	Anaheim, CA
Fentress County School District	Jamestown, TN
First Baptist Christian School	Mishawaka, IN
Flowing Wells School District 8	Tucson, AZ
Freedom Baptist Schools	Hudsonville, MI
Freeport Union School District	Freeport, NY
Golden Hills Seventh Day Adventist School	Bellevue, NE
Grace Lutheran School	Oshkosh, WI
Greenville Independent School District	Greenville, TX
Happy Valley Unified School District	Anderson, CA
Hayes Center School District	Hayes Center, NE
Jackson County School District	Hurley, MS Ocean Springs, MS
Jamul-Dulzura Union School District	Jamul, CA
Kingfisher Independent School District 7	Kingfisher, OK
Landmark Christian Academy	Louisville, KY
Lawton Community School District	Lawton, MI
Lea's Christian School	Hayward, CA
Litchfield Community School District	Litchfield, MI
Lutheran Church-Missouri Synod Pacific Southwest District	Irvine, CA
Maine School Administrative Distric #20	Fort Fairfield, ME
Marion County School District	Fairmont, WV
Mountain View School District	Kingsley, PA
Munday Independent School District	Munday, TX
Nassau County School District	Bryceville, FL Fernandina Beach, FL Greenacres City, FL Hilliard, FL Yulee, Fl
Oden School District 43	Oden, AR
Orting School District 344	Orting, WA
Oshkosh School District	Oshkosh, WI
Oxford School District	Oxford, MS
Palm Beach County School District	Palm Beach County, FL
Perrydale School District 21	Amity, OR
Piedmont City School District	Piedmont, AL

Pinconning Area Schools	Pinconning, MI
Plainfield School District	Plainfield, NJ
Redeemer Montessori School	Irving, TX
Rocky Mount Academy	Rocky Mount, NC
Roseville City School District	Roseville, CA
Saginaw Public School District	Saginaw, MI
St. Mark Lutheran School	North Tonawanda, NY
St. Mark Methodist School	Mobile, AL
St. Mark's Academy	Cocoa, FL
Saugus Union School District	Saugus, CA
Shaw School District	Shaw, MS
Shelbyville School District 4	Shelbyville, IL
Shoreline Christian School	Shoreline, WA
South Rock Creek School District 032	Shawnee, OK
Steel Valley School District	Munhall, PA
Stockbridge Community School District	Stockbridge, MI
Sulphur Rock School District	Sulphur Rock, AR
Three Angels SDA School	St. Joseph, MO
Trinity Lutheran School	San Diego, CA
Trinity Lutheran School	Greeley, CO
Vallejo City Unified School District	Vallejo, CA
Wayne Highlands School District	Lakewood, PA
Westside Elementary School District	Five Points, CA
White Rock School District	Mc Loud, OK
Whitley County Consolidated School District	Columbia City, IN
Whitney Independent School District	Whitney, TX
Zion Lutheran School	Kearney, NE

Appendix D

Schools Participating in Boehm–3 Spanish Edition, Standardization Testing

Fall

Schools	City and State
Archdiocese of San Antonio	San Antonio, TX
Buhl School District 412	Buhl, ID
Diocese of Brownsville Schools	Alamo, TX
Jamestown City School District	Jamestown, NY
Mohawk Valley School District	Roll, AZ
Orange County Public School District	Orlando, FL
Socorro Independent School District	El Paso, TX
Springdale School District	Springdale, AR
Yarbrough Public School District	Goodwell, OK

Spring

Schools	City and State
Charleston County School District	North Charleston, SC
Dallas Independent School District	Dallas, TX
Dickinson Independent School District	Dickinson, TX
Freeport Union School District	Freeport, NY
Gulfport School District	Gulfport, MS
Lehigh Valley Lutheran School	Northampton, PA
Madera Unified School District	Madera, CA
Oconee County School District	Walhalla, SC
Palm Beach County School District	Belle Glade, FL

Appendix E

Concepts in Order of Difficulty by Grade

English — Fall

	K	1	2
Least Difficult	through	top	top
	always	always	whole
	top	through	last
	different	first	always
	few	front	end
	whole	different	through
	front	last	first
	starting	few	row
	away	whole	few
	first	end	front
	over	bottom	match
	match	away	behind
	farthest	corner	farthest
	row	match	above
	behind	behind	bottom
	corner	farthest	away
	end	over	alike
	side	starting	starting
	bottom	row	different
	most	part	most
	part	alike	side
	alike	side	pair
	last	below	corner
	above	above	part
	below	most	next
	as many	second	never
	half	as many	over
	center	third	half
	next	never	third
	widest	next	second
	between	half	as many
	pair	pair	below
	beginning	center	separated
	every	widest	beginning
	other	other	backward
	never	separated	widest
	backward	between	center
	medium-sized	beginning	before
	forward	before	between
	separated	backward	other
	some	least	medium-sized
	before	forward	equal
	second	medium-sized	least
	third	every	forward
	least	right	every
	right	equal	skip
	left	skip	right
	equal	left	some
	fewest	some	left
Most Difficult	skip	fewest	fewest

English — Spring

	K	1	2
Least Difficult	through	top	last
	always	first	row
	top	last	top
	first	always	whole
	few	through	always
	different	few	end
	whole	different	through
	away	whole	first
	front	end	few
	end	farthest	front
	starting	away	away
	bottom	front	side
	last	row	farthest
	side	side	part
	row	corner	bottom
	farthest	starting	second
	over	most	match
	match	match	behind
	part	behind	different
	corner	bottom	below
	most	below	above
	above	alike	every
	behind	over	alike
	as many	third	third
	below	part	starting
	alike	every	most
	every	second	separated
	pair	above	never
	half	as many	corner
	widest	never	over
	third	half	as many
	never	pair	half
	center	separated	beginning
	other	center	center
	second	widest	between
	beginning	beginning	pair
	next	between	before
	between	before	backward
	backward	other	equal
	medium-sized	backward	other
	before	medium-sized	least
	separated	next	widest
	forward	equal	medium-sized
	some	least	forward
	least	forward	next
	right	skip	skip
	left	some	some
	equal	right	right
	skip	left	left
Most Difficult	fewest	fewest	fewest

Spanish — Fall

	K	1	2
Least Difficult	debajo	arriba	siempre
	arriba	siempre	línea
	iguales	debajo	más
	a tráves	a tráves	primer
	empezando	línea	más lejos
	línea	más alto	par
	más abajo	en frente	arriba
	detrás	iguales	iguales
	más alto	empezando	en medio de
	en frente	detrás	pocos
	siempre	más lejos	completo
	primer	completo	último
	sobre	primer	a tráves
	pocos	último	separados
	diferente	pocos	izquierda
	completo	esquina	empezando
	más lejos	diferente	esquina
	nunca	más abajo	más alto
	tantos...como	sobre	al lado
	en medio de	separados	nunca
	el centro	nunca	en frente
	par	par	diferente
	esquina	tantos...como	retirado
	más	más	igual
	al lado	en medio de	mitad
	cada	al lado	mediano
	mas ancha	final	tantos...como
	retirado	retirado	final
	último	parte	segundo
	mitad	más ancha	debajo
	hacen juego	el centro	más abajo
	final	menos	parte
	mediano	igual	tercer
	separados	hacen juego	hacia atrás
	parte	cada	el centro
	menos	mitad	más cerca
	igual	mediano	hacen juego
	algunos	otro	menos
	sáltense	más cerca	empezando
	otro	antes	inclinado
	antes	tercer	sobre
	derecha	empezando	algunos
	inclinado	segundo	más ancha
	izquierda	algunos	otro
	la menor cantidad	derecha	cada
	empezando	izquierda	antes
	hacia atrás	inclinado	derecha
	segundo	hacia atrás	sáltense
	mas cerca	la menor cantidad	detrás
Most Difficult	tercer	sáltense	la menor cantidad

Spanish — Spring

	K	1	2
Least Difficult	detrás	siempre	arriba
	arriba	en frente	en frente
	a través	detrás	debajo
	iguales	línea	empezando
	más alto	iguales	más abajo
	línea	a través	tercer
	debajo	arriba	último
	siempre	primer	siempre
	más abajo	último	línea
	completo	debajo	pocos
	pocos	empezando	diferente
	más lejos	completo	primer
	en frente	más alto	detrás
	primer	pocos	al lado
	empezando	diferente	iguales
	diferente	más	completo
	al lado	al lado	par
	esquina	tantos...como	más alto
	sobre	más lejos	más lejos
	tantos...como	final	final
	último	esquina	mediano
	en medio de	más abajo	separados
	más	separados	mitad
	el centro	par	el centro
	separados	nunca	nunca
	menos	menos	en medio de
	más ancha	parte	esquina
	retirado	mitad	igual
	mediano	segundo	a través
	más cerca	igual	más
	par	otro	segundo
	final	retirado	sobre
	mitad	en medio de	tantos...como
	parte	sobre	retirado
	hacen juego	mediano	más ancha
	igual	tercer	parte
	nunca	más ancha	cada
	otro	el centro	menos
	algunos	antes	antes
	tercer	cada	más cerca
	derecha	hacen juego	hacen juego
	segundo	empezando	otro
	izquierda	más cerca	empezando
	antes	algunos	algunos
	cada	hacia atrás	derecha
	la menor cantidad	derecha	hacia atrás
	inclinado	la menor cantidad	la menor cantidad
	empezando	izquierda	izquierda
	hacia atrás	inclinado	inclinado
Most Difficult	sáltense	sáltense	sáltense

References

Ault, R.L., Cromer, C.C., & Mitchell, C. (1977). The Boehm Test of Basic Concepts: A three-dimensional version. *Journal of Educational Research, 70*(4), 186–188.

Bagnato, S.J., Neisworth, J.T., & Munson, S.M. (1989). *Linking developmental assessment and early intervention: Curriculum based prescriptions* (2nd ed.). Rockville, MD: Aspen.

Beech, M.A. (1980, April). *Concurrent and predictive validity of the Boehm Test of Basic Concepts.* Paper presented at the Annual International Convention of the Council for Exceptional Children, Philadelphia, PA.

Beech, M.A. (1981). Concurrent validity of the Boehm Test of Basic Concepts. *Learning Disability Quarterly, 4,* 53–60.

Blai, B. (1973). Concept learning-mastery in Harcum Junior College Laboratory Nursery School/Kindergarten. *Psychology, 10,* 35–36.

Blewitt, P. (1982). Word meaning acquisition in young children: A review of theory and research. In H.W. Reese & L.P. Lipsitt (Eds.), *Advances in Child Development and Behavior* (Vol. 17, pp. 139–195). New York: Academic Press.

Boehm, A.E. (1967). The development of comparative concepts in primary school children (Doctoral dissertation, Columbia University, 1966). *Dissertation Abstracts International, 27,* 4109B. (Published as the Boehm Test of Basic Concepts).

Boehm, A.E. (1971). *Boehm Test of Basic Concepts (manual).* New York: The Psychological Corporation.

Boehm, A.E. (1976). *Boehm Resource Guide for Basic Concept Teaching.* New York: The Psychological Corporation.

Boehm, A.E. (1982). Assessment of basic concepts. In K.D. Paget & B.A. Bracken (Eds.), *The Psychoeducational assessment of preschool children* (pp. 145–161). New York: Grune & Stratton.

Boehm, A.E. (1986) *Parent teacher conference report.* San Antonio, TX: The Psychological Corporation.

Boehm, A.E. (1991). Assessment of children's knowledge of basic concepts. In C.R. Reynolds & R.W. Kamphaus (Eds.), *Handbook of psychological and educational assessment of children: Intelligence and achievement* (pp. 654–670). New York: The Guilford Press.

Boehm, A.E. (2000) Assessment of basic relational concepts. In B.A. Bracken (Ed), *The psychological assessment of preschool children* (pp. 186–203). Needham Heights, MA: Allyn & Bacon.

Boehm, A.E., Classon, B., & Kelly, (1986). *Preschool teachers' spoken use of basic concepts.* Unpublished manuscript. Teachers College, Columbia University.

Boehm, A.E. & Slater, B.R. (1981). *Cognitive Skills Assessment Battery* (2nd ed.). New York: Teachers College Press.

Boehm, A.E., Kaplan, C.H., & Preddy, D. (1980). How important are basic concepts to instruction: Validation of the Boehm Test of Basic Concepts. Unpublished paper, Teachers College, Columbia University, New York.

Bracken, B.A. (1986). Incidence of basic concepts in the directions of five commonly used American tests of intelligence. *School Psychology International, 7,* 1–10.

Bracken, B.A. (1998). *Bracken Basic Concept Scale–Revised.* San Antonio, Texas: The Psychological Corporation.

Bracken, B.A. & Cato, L.A. (1986). Rate of conceptual development among deaf preschool and primary children as compared to a matched group of nonhearing impaired children. *Psychology in the Schools, 23,* 95–99.

Brown, D. (1976). Validation of the Boehm Test of Basic Concepts (Doctoral dissertation, University of Wisconsin, 1976). *Dissertation Abstracts International, 36,* 4338A.

Busch, R.F. (1980). Predicting first-grade reading achievement. *Learning Disability Quarterly, 3,* 38–48.

Campbell, D.T., & Fiske, D.W. (1959). Convergent and discriminant validation by the multitrait-multimethod matrix. *Psychological Bulletin, 56,* 81–105.

Caton, H.R. (1976a). The development and evaluation of a tactile analogue to the Boehm Test of Basic Concepts (Doctoral dissertation, University of Kentucky). *Dissertation Abstracts International, 36,* 6596A.

Caton, H.R. (1976b). *The tactile test of basic concepts.* Louisville, KY: American Printing House for the Blind.

Caton, H.R. (1977). The development and evaluation of a tactile analogue to the Boehm Test of Basic Concepts, Form A. *Journal of Visual Impairment and Blindness, 71,* 382–386.

Central Arkansas Education Center. (1972). *The detection and remediation of deficiencies in verbal understanding of first grade students.* Little Rock, AR: (ERIC Document Reproduction Service No. ED 080 967/EC 00 705)

Chin, J.L. (1975). The development of basic relational concepts in educable mentally retarded children (Doctoral dissertation, Teachers College, Columbia University, 1975). *Dissertation Abstracts International, 35,* 2762A.

Clark, D.C. (1971). Teaching concepts in the classroom: A set of teaching prescriptions derived from experimental research. *Journal of Educational Psychology Monograph, 62,* 253–278.

Clark, E. (1983). Meaning and concepts. In P.H. Mussen (Series Ed.), T.H. Flavell & E.M. Markman (Vol. Eds.), *Handbook of child psychology, Vol. 3: Cognitive development* (pp. 787–840). New York: Wiley & Sons.

Clark, E.V. (1980). Here's the top: Nonlinguistic strategies in the acquisition of relational terms. *Child Development, 51,* 329–338.

Classon, B. (1988). Adult language input and children's acquisition of spatial/temporal relational terms. Unpublished doctoral dissertation, New York: Columbia University.

Classon, B.E., & Boehm, A.E. (1989). Adult language input and children's acquisition of spatial/temporal relational concept terms. Paper presented at the Biennial Meeting for the Society for Research in Child Development, Kansas City Missouri, April 1989.

Conner, P.G., & Chapman, R.S. (1985). The development of locative comprehension in Spanish. *Journal of Child Language, 12,* 109–123.

Crocker, L., & Algina, J. (1986). *An introduction to classical and modern test theory.* Austin, TX: Holt, Rinehart & Winston.

Cruz de Nason, O., Boehm, A.E., & Shepherd, M. (1987). The effects of systematic instruction of basic relational concepts on the performance of Puerto Rican first grade children from low income families. Unpublished paper, Teachers College, Columbia University.

Cummings, J.A., & Nelson, R.B. (1980). Basic concepts in oral directions of group achievement tests. *Journal of Educational Research, 73,* 259–261.

Davis, J. (1974). Performance of young hearing-impaired children on a text of basic concepts. *Journal of Speech and Hearing Research, 17,* 342–351.

de Villiers, J.G., & de Villiers, P.A. (1978). *Language acquisition.* Boston: Harvard University Press.

Dickie, D.C. (1980). Performance of severely and profoundly hearing impaired children on aural/oral and total communication presentations of the Boehm Test of Basic Concepts (Doctoral dissertation, Michigan State University, 1980). *Dissertation Abstracts International, 40,* 6227–6228A.

DiNapoli, N., Kagedan-Kage, S.M., & Boehm, A.E. (1980). *Basic concept acquisition in learning-disabled children.* (ERIC Document Reproduction Service No. ED 240 718)

Elliott, C.D. (1990). *Differential Ability Scales.* San Antonio, TX: The Psychological Corporation.

Erickson, J.G., & Inglesias, A. (1989). Assessment of communication disorders in non-English proficient children. In O. Taylor (Ed.), *The nature of communication disorders in culturally and linguistically diverse populations* (pp. 181–217). San Diego, CA: College-Hill Press.

Estes, G., Harris, J., Moers, F., & Wodrich, D. (1976). Predictive validity of the Boehm Test of Basic Concepts for achievement in first grade. *Educational and Psychological Measurement, 36,* 1031–1035.

Flanagan, D.P., Alfonso, V.C., Kaminer, T., & Rader, D.E. (1995). Incidence of basic concepts in the directions of new and recently revised American intelligence tests for preschool children. *School Psychology International, 16*, 345–364.

French, L.A., & Nelson, K. (1985). *Young children's knowledge of relational terms: Some ifs, ors, or buts.* New York: Springer-Verlag.

Glutting, J.J., Kelly, M.S., Boehm, A.E., & Burnett, T.R. (1989). Stability and predictive validity of the Boehm Test of Basic Concepts-Revised among black kindergartners. *Journal of School Psychology, 27*, 365–371.

Goldberg, M.L. (1975). *Effects of various approaches to beginning reading for disadvantaged children: Report of the project.* (Mimeo). New York Center for Urban Education.

Harris, A.J., & Jacobson, M.D. (1982). *Basic reading vocabularies.* New York: Macmillan Publishing.

Hart, B., & Risley, T.R., (1995). *Meaningful differences in the everyday experiences of young American children.* Baltimore, MD: Paul H. Brooks.

Herman, D.L., Huesing, P.D., Levett, C.A., & Boehm, A.E. (1973). *A follow-up study of the BTBC standardization sample: Correlation with later measures of achievement.* Paper presented at the meeting of the National Association of School Psychologists, New York, NY.

Houck, C.K., Biskin, D.S., & Regetz, J. (1973). A comparison of urban and rural reliability estimates for the Boehm Test of Basic Concepts. *Psychology in the Schools, 10*, 430–432.

Johnson, D.D., & Pearson, P.D. (1978). *Teaching reading vocabulary.* New York: Holt, Rinehart & Winston.

Johnston, J.R., & Slobin, D.I. (1979). The development of locative expressions in English, Italian, Serbo-Croatian, and Turkish. *Journal of Child Language, 6*, 529–545.

Kaplan, C.H. (1979). A developmental analysis of children's direction-following behavior in grades K–5 (Doctoral dissertation, Columbia University, New York, 1978). *Dissertation Abstracts International, 40*, 2615A.

Kaplan, C.H., & White, N.A. (1980). Children's direction-following behavior in grades K–5. *Journal of Educational Research, 74*, 43–48.

Kaufman, A. (1978). The importance of basic concepts in the individual assessment of preschool children. *Journal of School Psychology, 16*, 207–211.

Kaufman, A.S., & Kaufman, N.L. (1983). *Kaufman Assessment Battery for Children.* Circle Pines, MN: American Guidance Service.

Kavale, K.A. (1982). A comparison of learning disabled and normal children on the Boehm Test of Basic Concepts. *Journal of Learning Disabilities, 15*, 160–161.

Kintsch, W. (1998). *Comprehension: A paradigm for cognition.* Cambridge: Cambridge University Press.

Kirk, S.A., McCarthy, J.J., & Kirk, W.D. (1982). *Illinois Test of Psycholinguistic Abilities.* Champaign, IL: Univesity of Illinois Press.

Klausmeier, H.J. (1976). Cognitive development during the school years. In J.R. Levin & V.L. Allen (Eds.), *Cognitive learning in children: Theories and strategies* (pp. 5–29). New York Academic Press.

Klausmeier, H.J. (1992). Concept learning and concept teaching. *Educational Psychologist, 27(3)*, 267–286.

Kuczaj. S.A., & Maratsos, M.P. (1975). On the acquisition of front, back, and side. *Child Development, 46*, 202–210.

Levin, J.R., Henderson, B., Levin, A.M., & Hoffer, G.L., (1975). Measuring knowledge of basic concepts by disadvantaged preschoolers. *Psychology in the Schools, 12*, 132–139.

Lidz, C.S. (1983). Issues in assessing preschool children. In K.D. Paget & B.A. Bracken (Eds.), *The psychological assessment of preschool children* (pp. 17–27). New York: Grune & Stratton.

Lidz, C.S. (1991). *Practitioner's guide to dynamic assessment.* New York: Guilford Press.

McCarthy, D. (1970). *McCarthy Scales of Children's Abilities*. San Antonio, TX: The Psychological Corporation.

McGrew, K.S., & Flanagan, D.P. (1998). The intelligence test desk reference (ITDR). Needham Heights, MA: Allyn & Bacon.

Meissner, J.A. (1973). The communication of relational concepts by inner city children (Doctoral dissertation, Teachers College, Columbia University, 1972). *Dissertation Abstracts International, 33*, 2794B.

Meissner, J.A. (1975). Use of relational concepts by inner city children. *Journal of Educational Psychology, 67*, 22–29.

Meissner, J.A. (1978). Judgment of clue adequacy by kindergarten and second grade children. *Developmental Psychology, 14*, 18–23.

Mickelson, N.I., & Galloway, C.G. (1973). Verbal concepts of Indian and non-Indian School Beginners. *Journal of Educational Research, 67*, 55–56.

Milian, M. (1996). Knowledge of basic concepts of young students with visual impairments who are monolingual or bilingual. *Journal of Visual Impairment and Blindness, 90*, 386–398.

Naglieri, J.A. (1996). *Naglieri Nonverbal Ability Test® — Multilevel Form*. San Antonio, TX: The Psychological Corporation.

Nason, F. O. (1986). Systematic instruction of basic relational concepts: Effects on the acquisition of concept knowledge and of language and mathematics achievement of Puerto Rican first graders from low-income families. Unpublished doctoral dissertation, Teachers College, Columbia University.

Moers F., & Harris J. (1978). Instruction in basic concepts and first grade achievement. *Psychology in the Schools, 15*, 84–86.

Nelson, R.B., & Cummings, J.A. (1981) Basic concept attainment of educable mentally handicapped children: Implications for teaching concepts. *Education and Training of Mentally Retarded, 16*, 303–306.

Nurss, J. R., & McGauvran, M. E. (1986). *Metropolitan Readiness Tests* (5th ed.). San Antonio, TX: Harcourt Educational Measurement.

Palardy, T.J. (1973). The impact of an intense program of spatial and temporal concepts on the measured intelligence of pre-school children (Doctoral dissertation, Ohio State University, 1973). *Dissertation Abstracts International, 34*, 2176–2177A.

Paterson Board of Education, New Jersey. (1971). Dale Avenue School early childhood education center project. (ERIC Document Reproduction Service No. ED 089 498/EC 061 442)

Patterson, M.C. (1981). Performance of Hutter children in English and Hutterish versions of the Boehm Test of Basic Concepts. *Dissertation Abstracts International, 41*, 2987.

Peverly, S.T., & Kitzen, K.R. (1998). Curriculum-based assessment of reading skills: Considerations and caveats for school psychologists. *Psychology in the Schools, 35*(1) pp. 29–47.

Piaget, J. (1929). *The child's conception of the world*. New York: Harcourt Brace.

Pianta, R.C., Nimetz, S.L., & Bennett, E. (1997). Mother-child relationships, teacher–child relationships, and school outcomes in preschool and kindergarten. *Early Childhood Research Quarterly, 12*, 263–280.

Piersel, W.C., & McAndrews, T. (1982). Concept acquisition and school progression: An examination of the Boehm Test of Basic Concepts. *Psychological Reports, 50*, 783–786.

Piersel, W.C., Plake, B.S., Reynolds, C.R., & Harding, R. (1982). Bias in content validity on the Boehm Test of Basic Concepts for White and Mexican-American children. *Contemporary Educational Psychology, 7*, 181–189.

Piersel, W.C., & Reynolds, C.R. (1981). Factorial validity of item classification on the Boehm Test of Basic Concepts (BTBC), Forms A and B. *Educational and Psychological Measurement, 41*, 579–5832.

Preddy, D., Boehm, A.E., & Shepherd, M.J. (1984). PBCB: A norming of the Spanish translation of the Boehm Test of Basic Concepts. *Journal of School Psychology, 22*, 407–413.

Reynolds, C.R., & Piersel, W.C. (1983). Multiple aspects of bias on the Boehm Test of Basic Concepts (Forms A & B) for White and Mexican-American children. *Journal of Psychoeducational Assessment, 1,* 135–142.

Rosenbluth, A.R. (1976). The feasibility of test translation between unrelated languages English and Navajo. *TESOL Quarterly, 10,* 33–43.

Seifert, H., & Schwarz, I. (1991). Treatment effectiveness of large group concept instruction with Head Start students. *Language, Speech, and Hearing Services in Schools, 22,* 60–64.

Seigler, R.S. (1998). *Children's thinking* (3rd ed.). Upper Saddle River, NJ: Prentice Hall.

Smith, E.F. (1986a). The validity of the Boehm Test of Basic Concepts. *British Journal of Educational Psychology, 56,* 332–344.

Smith, E.F. (1986b). The Boehm Test of Basic Concepts: An English standardization. *British Journal of Educational Psychology, 56,* 197–200.

Spector, C.C. (1977). Concept comprehension of normal kindergarten children with deviant syntactic development (Doctoral dissertation, New York University, New York, 1977). *Dissertation Abstracts International, 38,* 2096A.

Spector, C.C. (1979). The Boehm Test of Basic Concepts: Exploring the test results for cognitive deficits. *Journal of Learning Disabilities, 12,* 564–567.

Steinbauer, E., & Heller, M.S. (1978). The Boehm Test of Basic Concepts as a predictor of academic achievement in grades 2 and 3. *Psychology in the Schools, 15,* 357–360.

Steinert, M.C. (1978). Construct and criterion-related validity of the Boehm Test of Basic Concepts. Unpublished dissertation, Kent State University.

Stott, D.H., McDermott, P.A., Green, L.F., & Francis, J. (1988a). *Learning Behaviors Scale: Research Edition Manual.* San Antonio, TX: The Psychological Corporation.

Stott, D.H., McDermott, P.A., Green, L.F., & Francis, J. (1988b). *Study of Children's Learning Behaviors: Research Edition Manual.* San Antonio, TX: The Psychological Corporation.

Taylor, S.F., Franckenpohl, H., & White, C.E. (1979). A revised core vocabulary. In S.E. Taylor, H. Franckenpohl, C.E. White, B.W. Nicroroda, C.L. Browning, & E.B. Birsner (Eds.), *EDL core vocabularies in reading, mathematics, sciences, and social studies.* New York: EDL/McGraw-Hill.

Tennyson, R.D., & Park, O. (1980). The teaching of concepts: A review of instructional design research literature. *Review of Educational Research, 50,* 55–70.

Tennysson, C.L., & Cocchiarella, M.J. (1986). An empirically based instructional design theory for teaching concepts. *Review of Educational Research, 56,* 40–71.

Thorndike, R.L., Hagen, E.P., & Sattler, J.M. (1986). *Stanford-Binet Intelligence Scale: Fourth Edition.* Chicago: Riverside.

Wechsler, D. (1967). *Wechsler Preschool and Primary Scale of Intelligence.* San Antonio, TX: The Psychological Corporation.

Wechsler, D. (1989). *Wechsler Preschool and Primary Scale of Intelligence–Revised.* San Antonio, TX: The Psychological Corporation.

Wiig, E.H., & Semel, E.M. (1976). *Language disabilities in children and adolescents.* Columbus, OH: Charles E. Merrill.

Woodcock, R.W., & Johnson, M.B. (1989). *Woodcock-Johnson Psycho-Educational Battery–Revised.* Allen, TX: DLM Teaching Resources.

Ysseldyke, J.E., & Thurlow, M.L. (1984). Assessment practices in special education: adequacy and appropriateness. *Educational Psychologist, 19,* 123–136.

Zhou, Z., & Boehm, A.E. (in press). American and Chinese children's knowledge of basic relational concepts. *School Psychology International, 21*(4), pp. 243–259.

Zucker, S., & Riordan, J. (1988). Concurrent validity of new and revised conceptual language measures. *Psychology in the Schools, 25,* 252–256.